# BIG **FISH** SMALL **POND**

TIM BADEN

Fulton Books
Meadville, PA

Published by Fulton Books 2024

ISBN 979-8-89427-492-8 (paperback)
ISBN 979-8-89427-493-5 (digital)

Printed in the United States of America

# INTRODUCTION

*1968*

In the quiet, small Appalachian town of Longstreth, nestled among rolling hills and whispering pines, I spent my childhood days. Our modest home, a refuge from life's storms, stood as a testament to my mother's resilience. She had divorced my abusive father when I was twelve, freeing us from his dark shadow. Raising the three of us on her own was a struggle, but we were better off than before. With four brothers and our loyal mutt, Tippy, I reveled in the simple pleasures of rural life.

Rubber boots adorned my feet, and a towel became my makeshift superhero cape. I'd dash through trees and hills, imagining daring rescues and epic battles against imaginary foes. The world beyond our small town seemed distant and irrelevant. Here, in the embrace of nature, I found solace.

My brother Fred had joined the Army and been shipped off to Korea, a million miles away. The rest of us three brothers were left to utter in rectitude.

But one frigid January night, fate intervened. We huddled downstairs by the fuel oilstove, seeking warmth. The loft, our usual sleeping quarters, lay abandoned. The heater's float malfunctioned, spilling fuel beneath the stove and into the closet under the stairs. Flames erupted, devouring our escape route—the very steps that would have led us to safety.

I awoke to smoke, disoriented, and gasping. My lungs rebelled against the acrid air. "Fire!" I shouted, my voice raw. Mom and my brothers stumbled from their slumber, their eyes wide with fear. Together, we stumbled outside, coughing and blinking against the haze. But Mom and my brother Jeff, their love for our home unwavering, charged back into the inferno to battle the flames.

My younger brother, Tom, and I watched from the neighbor's porch, our hearts pounding. The Fire Department, eight miles away, became our beacon of hope. Minutes stretched into eternity as we waited. Finally, they arrived—a team of heroes clad in turnout gear, their faces determined.

They moved with precision, like a symphony of bravery. Water hoses danced, spraying arcs of salvation. The flames retreated, defeated, but not without a fight. Our home, once a sanctuary, now lies in ruins. Mom collapsed, tears streaming down her soot-streaked face. The firemen worked tirelessly, their rhythm echoing the storm that had consumed our lives.

# CHAPTER 1

# SUMMER IN THE HILLS

*1972*

In the heart of Ohio, where rolling hills meet the horizon, there lies a railway steeped in history—the Hocking Valley Railway. Its iron tracks wind through lush forests, past quaint towns, and over bridges that echo with the memories of countless journeys.

But time is a relentless conductor. By 1930, the Hocking Valley Railway had yielded to the Chesapeake and Ohio (C&O), its legacy woven into the steel sinews of a larger network. Passenger service faded, replaced by the steady pulse of freight trains. The "Nelsonville Turn" became a solitary echo, its wheels tracing memories along the Monday Creek Branch.

Yet hope never abandoned those tracks. In 1972, three visionaries—Frank, Ted, and Jerry—breathed life into the old Monday Creek Branch. They christened it the Hocking Valley Scenic Railway (HVSR). Their dream? To resurrect the past, to let steam locomotives breathe fire once more. They salvaged three Erie Railroad coaches, stitching them together like a patchwork quilt of nostalgia.

And then fate intervened. The Monday Creek line, slated for scrap, found its saviors. The HVSR acquired it just in time, saving the iron veins that once pulsed with industry. A 1916 Lake Superior & Ishpeming locomotive, No. 33, joined their ranks. Its whistle echoed across the hills, announcing a new era.

The first "station" was humble—a tarp stretched between poles. Later, a donated building stood sentinel. But the true gem was the original Hocking Valley Railway order office, transplanted from Lancaster. Passengers arrived, their eyes wide with wonder, as No. 33 puffed and hissed. The seasons turned, and the locomotive retreated to the C&O's Parson Yard roundhouse, awaiting spring's call.

In the quiet hills of Longstreth, Ohio, nestled between the rugged peaks of Appalachia, life unfolded at its own pace. Our small town, home to about a hundred souls, clung to existence like the stubborn roots of an ancient oak. Accessible only by the winding Carbon-Hill Buchtel Road, Longstreth was a place where time seemed to stretch and yawn, reluctant to move forward.

I remember those days vividly—the days when I was fourteen, and the world was both vast and intimate. Money was scarce, but hand-me-downs were abundant. We patched our jeans and stitched our dreams together, weaving a tapestry of resilience and hope. Longstreth, named during the coal boom of the 1900s, held secrets in its soil—stories etched into the very rocks that cradled our homes.

The ball diamond stood as a relic of bygone summers, where the crack of wooden bats echoed through the valley. Baseball was our passion, and we played with the fervor of champions, even if our victories were measured in laughter and scraped knees. The green pond, a tranquil oasis, lay at the heart of our town. Its waters mirrored the sky, and generations of children learned to swim in its embrace. The Y-shaped railroad tracks, their iron veins coursing through the land, created the pond—a testament to human ingenuity and nature's whimsy.

And then there was Monday Creek, winding lazily through the valley like an old storyteller recounting forgotten tales. Its waters whispered secrets to the sycamores and maples, and we listened, our bare feet dipped in its coolness. Sometimes, when the sun dipped below the hills, we'd gather by the creek, our faces painted with fire-flies, and share our dreams. Dreams of escape, of adventure beyond the hills, of places where the world was louder and faster.

But Longstreth held us close; its quietude was a balm for our restless souls. We knew every neighbor, every creaky porch swing, and every patch of wildflowers that bloomed defiantly along the road. The county road, our lifeline, wound through the hills like a silver thread connecting us to the outside world. It carried whispers of distant cities, of bustling streets, and of skyscrapers that touched the clouds. Yet we remained rooted, our hearts entwined with the soil, our stories etched into the very fabric of Longstreth.

Those days—the mixed blessings of simplicity and yearning—shaped us. We grew strong, not in wealth or grandeur, but in resilience and kinship. Longstreth, our hidden gem, taught us that life need not be loud to be meaningful. It was in the quiet moments—the rustle of leaves, the taste of blackberries, the laughter shared on warm summer nights—that we found our true wealth.

I first met Ted when I spotted a little railroad car chugging along the tracks past the serene green pond. Its one-cylinder engine emitted a rhythmic *chug-chug* sound as it progressed, leaving a trail of nostalgia in its wake. The sun dipped low, casting long shadows across the rusty rails.

Curiosity tugged at me. What was this relic doing here? Who were the mysterious men accompanying it? I decided to follow the tracks, my faithful wire terrier, Tippie, trotting alongside me. Tippie had wandered into our lives as a stray puppy, and our bond was unbreakable. His wiry coat and unwavering loyalty made him my constant companion.

As I walked the old, abandoned Y Spurr tracks, I rounded a corner and came upon the source of the clanging tolls. Two men—determined and weathered—were prying at a spike embedded in a railroad tie. Their spike puller strained against the rusted metal. I approached, my heart racing.

One of the men extended his hand, introducing himself as Ted. His grip was firm, and his eyes held a spark of adventure. I must have looked comical—a fourteen-year-old boy who appeared even younger—but Ted didn't seem to mind. He began weaving a tale of the past—the C and O Railroad that had once thrived on these very rails. Now, they lay abandoned, forgotten by time.

"We're forming the Hocking Valley Scenic Railway," Ted explained. His words hung in the air, promising adventure and history intertwined. I listened with intensity, captivated by the vision he painted—the restored cars, the scenic route, and the promise of steam-powered journeys.

Ted leaned in, sensing my eagerness. "Go home," he said, "ask your mom if you can ride the motor car down these tracks." His eyes twinkled. "You'll be part of something special."

I raced home, breathless with excitement. Mom raised an eyebrow when I burst through the door, but I spilled the story—the railroad car, Ted, and the invitation. She smiled, her eyes reflecting my own anticipation. "Yes," she said. "Go explore those tracks, my adventurous boy."

And so with Tippie by my side, I embarked on a journey beyond the green pond—a journey that would shape my teenage years, ignite my passion for trains, and introduce me to a cast of characters who became family. Ted, the man with stories etched into his wrinkles, became my mentor, and the Hocking Valley Scenic Railway became my second home.

The motor car rattled along the tracks, its wheels grinding against the rusty rails. I clung to the side, feeling the vibrations resonate through my bones. My trusted dog, Tippie, clings tightly to me. The pulse of the engine surged beneath me—a heartbeat of forgotten journeys and whispered secrets.

Ted sat across from me, his grin like sunlight breaking through storm clouds. His eyes sparkled with mischief and wisdom, a combination that made him instantly likable. Beside him, his partner—a quiet man with calloused hands—nodded in approval. They were the architects of this adventure, the stewards of a bygone era.

"Carbon Hill awaits," Ted announced, his voice carried away by the wind. "Every third tie must be solid. Inspection protocol." He pointed at the wooden crossbeams that held the rails in place. Years of neglect had taken their toll—the ties were like old bones, brittle and splintered.

I leaned out, watching the landscape blur past. The green canopy of trees enveloped us, and the scent of pine mingled with the metallic tang of the tracks. Tippie, my faithful terrier, sat at my feet, ears flapping in the breeze. He was as eager as I was, sensing the magic of this moment.

"Young blood," Ted said, leaning closer. "We need workers. Boys like you—strong, willing, hungry for adventure." His eyes bore into mine. "Cash money, son. Real wages."

I didn't hesitate. "Yes," I blurted out. "Count me in."

And just like that, I became part of the team—a ragtag crew of boys armed with hammers, spikes, and determination. We descended on the tracks like ants, replacing ties and hammering them into place. The sun beat down, sweat trickling into our eyes. But we laughed, sang, and shared stories—the camaraderie of labor binding us tighter than any iron rail.

Ted worked alongside us, sleeves rolled up, sweat staining his shirt. His partner—silent but steady—kept pace. They taught us the rhythm of the work, the art of aligning rails, and the satisfaction of a job well done. And when payday arrived, we lined up like soldiers, grinning as coins jingled in our pockets.

The wind continued to blow, carrying our laughter and dreams toward the horizon. We rebuilt the tracks, one tie at a time, weaving history back together. Carbon Hill welcomed us—the town's folks waving from porches, their eyes knowing. They'd seen the decline, the tracks fading into obscurity. Now, they watched us resurrect the past.

As the sun dipped low, casting long shadows, I stood on a freshly laid tie. Tippie sat beside me, tongue lolling. Ted clapped my shoulder, his grin wider than ever. "You're part of something timeless," he said. "A legacy."

And I believed him. The *chug, chug,* of the engine echoed my heartbeat—the rhythm of purpose, of connection. I looked down at the tracks, where they stretched beyond sight, disappearing into the unknown. Somewhere out there, other boys would take up the mantle, their hands gripping hammers and their hearts echoing our resolve.

And so the days of that summer passed as I worked with Ted and the crew. We worked from Nelsonville to Carbon Hill. I was becoming a man.

The sun hung low in the sky, casting long shadows across the tracks as our work train cars trundled along. Tippie, my loyal wire terrier, darted alongside us, his tail a blur of excitement. He loved these tracks—their rusty promise, the scent of adventure carried on the wind.

As we neared State Route 78, the work car slowed. One of the crew members leaped off, signaling the crossing. Tippie saw him and bound toward the road, ears flapping. His wiry coat glinted in the afternoon light. I watched, pride swelling in my chest. Tippie was more than a dog; he was my companion and my confidant.

And then it happened—a blur of metal, a screech of tires. A car, oblivious to our presence, struck Tippie. The impact sent him rolling down the road, a helpless bundle of fur. My heart clenched, and I screamed for help. But it was too late. Tippie lay still, eyes wide, life extinguished in an instant.

The driver had stopped, remorse etched on their faces. They knelt beside Tippie, but there was nothing to be done. Our faithful friend was gone. We buried him beside the tracks, the soil accepting him into its embrace. The crew stood in a circle, tears streaming down their weathered faces. We'd lost more than a dog; we'd lost a piece of our souls.

Ted, usually gruff and unyielding, wiped his eyes. "He was family," he murmured. "Tippie ran these rails with us. He knew every twist, every secret."

And so as the sun dipped below the horizon, we paid our respects. Tippie's grave was marked by a simple wooden cross, the tracks stretching beyond—a path he'd never run again. The wind whispered through the pines, carrying our grief away.

In the days that followed, the work continued. But the rhythm was different—Tippie's absence was a silent ache. We worked harder and hammered the spikes with renewed purpose. And when the motor car rumbled along those same tracks, I felt his presence—the *chug-chug* of the engine echoing his heartbeat.

Tippie had become part of the rails, woven into their history. His memory spurred us on, a reminder that even in loss, there was purpose. And as we laid each tie, we whispered his name—a tribute to the dog who'd run beside us, forever etched in the tracks of our hearts.

Summer was fading, and the air held a hint of autumn. The tracks, once overgrown and forgotten, now gleamed in anticipation. The behemoth of a steam engine, Engine No. 33, stood ready to reclaim its place on the line. Its iron frame bore the scars of time, a testament to decades of hauling ore trains for the Lake Superior & Ishpeming Railroad.

In 1916, No. 33 was born—a mechanical giant with a heart of fire. It pulled heavy loads through rugged terrain, its wheels pounding the rails, leaving echoes in the forests. But progress marched on, and by the late 1990s, the old engine faced retirement. That's when the High Valley Scenic Railway (HVSR) volunteers stepped in. They labored tirelessly, breathing life back into No. 33. By the early 1970s, the engine chugged once more, its smokestack billowing nostalgia.

The HVSR crew revealed this in their victory, but fate had more in store. In 2003, No. 33 found a new home with the Ohio Central Railroad. The restoration continued, and soon the behemoth roared back to life, its pistons pumping, wheels turning, and whistles echoing across the hills. It became a living relic, a bridge between the eras.

I remember that first ride—the rhythmic clang of the rails, the scent of coal, and the thrill of adventure. I sat in a passenger car, gazing out at the world rushing by. The engine hissed and groaned, as if sharing its secrets with the wind. I thought of the forgotten tracks we'd resurrected, the sweat-soaked days of labor, and the camaraderie of fellow rail enthusiasts.

Silently, I thanked the old engine. It had carried dreams, memories, and the weight of history. As we approached Carbon Hill, the town came alive. People lined the streets, faces lifted in awe. No. 33 rolled to a stop, steam enveloping us. The crowd cheered, and I knew—we hadn't just repaired rails; we'd rekindled a love affair with the past.

# CHAPTER 2

# GROWING UP NELSONVILLE STYLE

*1970s*

High school is a formative life experience that shapes us in ways beyond academics. It's a jostling bazaar of potential identities, where students encounter roles like jock, prep, or geek and choose (or are assigned) one that sticks with them for years to come. For some, high school shines like an enchanted kingdom, while for others, it's remembered as an endless hell of daily torments. Regardless, those years leave an emotional imprint that lingers throughout our lives. Your quiet existence in the corridors, seeking solace in shadows and the haunting melodies of your trombone.

And then there was Judy.

Judy, with her soft-spoken demeanor and eyes that held secrets, and I shared the same grade, our paths intersecting in the hallowed halls of the band room. She, too, kept her distance from the bustling crowds; her trumpet was an extension of her soul. Shyness clung to her like a delicate veil, but beneath it lay a beauty that transcended mere appearances.

We gravitated toward each other during band functions—the rhythm of our instruments weaving a silent symphony. Our notes danced, harmonizing in the twilight hours. And somewhere between trumpet blasts and clarinet trills, we became more than just fellow musicians. We became boyfriend and girlfriend, our hearts entwined like the ivy that clung to the school's brick walls.

Our romance unfolded like a gentle waltz. We held hands during football games, our fingers brushing against the fabric of our band uniforms. A stolen kiss behind the bleachers—a secret shared only with the fireflies that flickered in the warm Ohio nights. Our love was platonic and innocent, yet it carried the weight of unspoken promises.

But life, like a capricious conductor, changed the tempo. Our notes began to drift apart, the harmonies faltering. Perhaps it was the pressure of growing up—the cacophony of responsibilities drowning out our sweet melodies. Or maybe we were destined for different movements in this grand symphony.

We lost touch after high school, our connection fading like a fading chord. Yet Judy lingered in my thoughts—the ghostly refrain of our shared laughter, the way her eyes crinkled when she smiled. I'd glimpse her in the grocery store, her wedding ring glinting under fluorescent lights. She'd nod, a silent acknowledgment of our past, and I'd carry that memory with me like a cherished vinyl record.

As for me, I married too—several times, as life spun its unpredictable tunes. Each union brought its own melody: the passionate crescendo, the melancholic adagio, and the staccato of arguments and forgiveness. But Judy remained a lingering note—an unresolved chord that resonated in quiet moments.

Behind the quarter moon, the sky unfolded—a canvas of twilight and clouds. It bore the essence of October, though May's warmth clung to the air. Crisp and unsullied, it whispered the secrets of the first frost. Clouds stretched like downy pillows across the firmament, their edges brushing the horizon. Transverse currents carried them in a slow ballet choreographed by unseen hands.

The moon, a celestial spotlight, casts its glow outward. Its backside was illuminated, and it painted the sky with silver strokes, touching each cloud as if whispering forgotten tales. And despite the coolness, the air bore the freshness of newly mown grass—a paradox of seasons that hung in the balance.

In the small town of Nelsonville, nestled among rolling hills and surrounded by dense forests, there stood a firehouse—a place that held both danger and heroism. For me, it was more than just a building; it was a beacon of hope and a symbol of courage. You see, ever since our own house had been consumed by flames when I was a teenager, I'd harbored a secret dream: to become a firefighter.

The firehouse was my sanctuary. I'd sneak away from school, my heart pounding with excitement, and visit as often as I could. The smell of polished brass, the sound of boots clattering against the floor, and the camaraderie among the firefighters—it all fascinated me. They were like modern-day knights, battling dragons made of fire.

But life had other plans. During my last two years of high school, I found myself in an electronics class. There, amid circuit boards and soldering irons, I met Harry. He was a quiet guy, always focused on his work. We'd exchange nods and occasional smiles and become friends. Little did I know that our paths would intersect in a way that would change my life forever.

Harry, as it turned out, had a secret too. He was training to be a firefighter. His eyes would light up when he talked about it—the adrenaline rush, the teamwork, and the satisfaction of saving lives. One day, after class, he pulled me aside.

"Hey," he said, his voice low, "you ever thought about joining the fire department?"

I blinked, surprised. "Me? But I'm an electronics guy." Outside the firehouse, the scene shifted. Streetlights etched smooth black pavement, glistening like ice on a winter pond. Shadows danced—a nocturnal masquerade—as if the very lampposts and trees harbored secrets. The streets lay empty, save for sporadic vehicles that sliced through the darkness. Each headlight banished the shadows, revealing transient creatures that scurried into hiding. Harry grinned. "Doesn't matter. We need all kinds. Besides, you've got the heart for it."

And just like that, he became my mentor. He taught me the basics—the difference between a pumper truck and a ladder truck, how to handle a hose, and the importance of staying calm under pressure. I soaked it all in, fueled by a newfound determination. A dream that Harry helped bring to life.

When the fire department announced they were hiring, Harry vouched for me. "He's got potential," he told the chief. "Give him a shot."

And they did.

The firehouse was a place of secrets, where the clang of boots and the smell of polished brass masked the unspoken trials that awaited new recruits. For me, it was a dream realized—a chance to become a firefighter, to be part of the brotherhood that battled infernos and saved lives.

But the journey there was anything but glamorous. I was riding in the back compartment of the engine. The captain had put me there so as not to spark the wrath of the chief since I was supposed to stay at the firehouse as a probe to cover any other emergencies. I was hanging on to the equipment inside for dear life. The driver, seemingly intent on testing my resolve, hit every pothole and railroad track with precision. Each jolt sent shock waves through my body, rattling my bones and making me question my decision. They called it "shaking me up," and it was an understatement.

As we arrived at the scene, the fire truck screeched to a halt. The hazing began—the guys in the truck were testing my mettle. I longed for the safety of the firehouse, where I could hide from their poking and prodding. But there was no turning back now.

The captain peeked into the compartment, his eyes assessing. "Stay in here," he whispered, his voice a mix of caution and camaraderie. "The Chief's here."

I nodded, my heart pounding. The heavy, heat-resistant bunker suit weighed on me, a reminder of the responsibility I'd willingly taken on. I could smell the smoke billowing, flames dancing, and fear gnawing at my insides. But Harry's words echoed in my mind: "You've got the heart for it."

Inside the compartment, chaos reigned. Water sprayed, boots stomped, and the heat threatened to consume me. Yet alongside the fear, there was something else—an adrenaline-fueled determination. They fought as a team, pushing forward despite the intensity. And when they finally doused the flames, pulling a family to safety, I felt relieved that it was over.

The firehouse had transformed me—from a hesitant recruit to a firefighter who understood sacrifice, courage, and the weight of responsibility. As I returned to the firehouse, surrounded by my comrades, I realized that sometimes the most excruciating journeys led to the most profound discoveries. The hazing had forged me, bloody and shaken, and I would never look back.

So if you ever hear the wail of a fire truck or catch a glimpse of smoke on the horizon, remember this: somewhere in the midst of chaos, there's a firefighter who wears the heavy suit, may be in one of the compartments, and is bloody and bruised.

From then on, I was part of the brotherhood—the firefighters who risked their lives to protect others. And as I stood in that same firehouse, surrounded by my comrades, I realized that dreams could ignite even in the darkest of times. All it took was a spark—a connection forged in the flames.

Across the way, the funeral home's sign pulsed—a beacon of tranquility against the night's uncertainty. This was no ordinary hour; it was a life experience unforeseen, a chapter etched in the annals of time.

The fire station stood sentinel; its bricks steeped in history. Built in the early 1900s, it housed not only the Fire Department but also a cacophony of municipal functions. City Hall, police, auditors, and treasurers all crammed within its walls, their footsteps echoing through the corridors. Must and mildew cling to the air, a testament to decades of service.

Above the entrance, an illuminated sign proclaimed, "City Hall," its letters etched in time. The garage door, newly remodeled, groaned as it struggled upward—a relic from horse and buggy days. Once, two doors flung open, releasing steeds that galloped forward with the steam wagon, bells ringing in alarm. Volunteers scattered, summoned by the tolling chime, their duty etched in bravery.

But the horses were gone now, replaced by modern engines—pumpers and a ladder truck. They sat side by side, like miniature Tonka toys, squeezed into the bay. A fire run demanded precision: one truck at a time, lest they become entangled in their mechanical dance. The garage door, operated by hand, revealed their readiness—a symphony of red and chrome.

In the dayroom, a couch sagged under the weight of countless firefighters. Five lockers stood sentinels, each holding stories of bravery and camaraderie. And at the room's end, a table cradled the Plectron radio system—a pager ahead of its time, its static-laden messages echoing through the station.

The hose tower stood like a lookout, its brick facade weathered by time and duty. Fifty-foot lengths of cotton fire hose hung there, drying in the sun—a relic of an era when synthetic hoses were yet to be invented. Behind the dayroom, a wooden stairway, forgotten and veiled in cobwebs, wound upward. Its steps whispered the secrets of countless ascents, each one leading to the rooftop hatch, four stories high.

And atop that roof perched the red fire siren—a patrol of a different kind. Powered by a twenty-five-horse motor, it spun its unidirectional wail, echoing across the city of over five thousand souls. From each landing, pane glass windows framed views of the world below—the streets, the rooftops, and the lives unfolding in the shadow of the tower.

The steps clung to the brick walls, open to the void within. As you climbed, euphoria and foreboding danced—a precarious waltz. The city spread out beneath you, its heartbeat pulsing through the soles of your boots. You wondered if you might plummet like a fallen star in the night.

Across the street, the shoe factory hummed—a symphony of labor. Men and women, their faces etched with determination, toiled within the three-story brick building. Their lives were stitched into the very fabric of the shoes they crafted—meager wages exchanged for survival. Second shift, and the factory floor buzzed with purpose.

Assigned stations, like chess pieces on a board, held workers in their places. Shoes and boots took shape—their leather uppers, soles, and heels assembled with precision. Soon, they'd grace storefronts, their newness a stark contrast to the sweat-soaked hands that birthed them.

Amid the rhythmic clatter, a tiny girl sat—a paradox of fragility and strength. Her chair, cushioned with wood and unforgiving, anchored her to the sole-setting machine. It loomed like a mechanical beast, its needle poised to pierce flesh without remorse. She wiped her brow with a soiled towel, her gaze never leaving the task at hand.

Her hands, small but deft, guided the monster. The machine heaved and labored, its metallic jaws hungry for leather. Her short, dirty-blond hair was a halo of determination, tied back to avoid the gears' grasp. She moved with grace, a ballet dancer in a gritty theater, pulling each shoe from the maw just in time to slip another into its awaiting embrace.

Outside, the fire siren's wail continued—a distant cry that bridged the gap between the tower and the factory. The girl, Judy, stitched hope into every sole. And as the night deepened, the echoes of her labor reverberated—a symphony of survival, resilience, and the quiet heroism of ordinary lives, for it was Judy living her everyday life.

The fire station stood weathered and steadfast, its bricks etched with decades of service. Above the dayroom door, a large red bell hung—a sentry poised to sound the alarm. Its round form, like a dinner bell, commanded attention, and its chime echoed through the station.

Nelsonville, a small city, scraped together resources for its fire crew. A chief, a captain, two regular firefighters, and an extra firefighter formed the full-time team. Twenty-three volunteers bolstered their ranks, ready to tackle larger incidents. Around the clock, one person manned the station, a solitary guardian awaiting the call to action.

And then it came—the alarm bell's urgent cry. The Plectron paging system hummed to life, alerting the necessary responders. My heart raced as I sprinted across the bay floor, the waxed surface slippery beneath my boots. The day shift's meticulous care had left the glazed block gleaming, a testament to their dedication.

Earlier, in the police department dispatcher room, I'd conversed with the dispatcher. We discussed the prisoners—those confined to what we affectionately called "the Dungeon." But now, duty called. The communications room awaited, its phone a lifeline to the outside world.

As I entered the dayroom, adrenaline surged. The lockers loomed, their metal edges unforgiving. I stumbled, my shoulder colliding with the first locker door. Gritting my teeth, I righted myself. This was my initiation—a baptism by alarm bell.

This was my first fire run. Alone in the dayroom, the phone rang—a shrill cry that echoed through my bones. Dread washed over me. What awaited on the other end? A car crash? A raging inferno? Or perhaps a cat stranded on a pole, its desperate mews piercing the night?

I reached for the receiver, my mind racing. The seconds stretched into eternity. "Fire Department, what is your emergency?" My voice cracked, my heart pounding. The caller's excitement spilled through the line. "Fire!" they exclaimed.

My throat tightened as I stood in the fire station, surrounded by the familiar scent of bunker gear smoke and the distant hum of traffic. This was it—the moment of truth. Some firefighters boasted of their calm and bravery during their first solo call. But not me. Fear clenched my chest, and my knees threatened to buckle under the weight of responsibility—a burden I hadn't fully comprehended until now.

The alarm blared, jolting me from my thoughts, my heart racing. The caller's voice crackled through the receiver, urgency dripping from every word. "My car is on fire!" Panic surged within me. I blurted out, "I'll be right there," forgetting to ask for the address before hanging up.

As I rushed to the fire truck, adrenaline pumping, I realized my mistake. How could I respond without knowing where to go? But luck was on my side. The police dispatcher had been listening in.

He met me across the hall, relaying the relevant information—the address, the situation, and the desperate plea for help.

I climbed into the fire truck, my hands gripping the wheel. Fear still gnawed at my insides, but duty propelled me forward. Sirens wailed as we sped toward the scene, the weight of responsibility settling firmly on my shoulders. This was my first solo call, and I vowed to face it head-on, even if my knees threatened to give way. After all, lives depended on it.

The fire truck roared to life, its sirens wailing. As I raced toward the inferno, I knew this was my baptism by fire—a trial by flames. This car fire, once a stage for dreams and melodies, now dances with destruction. I had to act swiftly and decisively.

Amid the chaos, I found my purpose—the legacy of those who'd come before me. With trembling hands, I donned the rest of my gear, and as I stopped short of the fire, the car was fully engulfed with flames cracking and popping. The weight of history is settling on my shoulders. The night air crackled with urgency, and as I stepped into the inferno's glow, I vowed to protect and serve—a firefighter, no longer an outsider, but a guardian of Nelsonville's heart and soul.

Tim Raden, a Nelsonville, Ohio, fireman, is lowered to the ground after suffering from smoke inhalation. The fire Monday gutted the historic Stuart's Opera House downtown, destroying several other buildings. Six other firefighters were treated for smoke inhalation, and three received minor injuries from falling glass in the five-hour blaze.

*Akron Beacon Journal*

# CHAPTER 3

# LIFESAVERS

*1980*

The small crew of four sat in the dayroom of the firehouse at 29 Fayette Street, basking in the noonday sun gliding gently through the windows. They exchanged banter about the improving weather and speculated about the mysterious girl who had just walked past the duty apron. In their youthful arrogance, they believed that all women were drawn to them—after all, they were firefighters. But then, abruptly, the fire bell shattered the tranquility. Its urgent clang echoed through the station, jolting them from their idle chatter. Before 911 existed, each fire department had a dedicated call-in number wired to the phone system. The bell signaled an incoming emergency call, and the crew sprang into action, leaving behind their daydreams and bravado. The real work awaited them, and they rushed to answer the call, ready to face whatever danger lay ahead. One of the officers answered, and I saw him look up as he was talking and hand the phone to another firefighter. He walked to the front door that led outside. He looked up toward the center of the city and said in an almost ghostly voice, "The town is on fire. Everyone ran to the truck bay and to their assigned equipment. The dispatcher for the day pushed the button on the plectron system to alert the off-duty firefighters and volunteer firefighters of the approaching catastrophe. The dispatcher alerted all available firefighters, both on and off duty, about the structure fire in downtown Nelsonville. The urgency was palpable as they rushed to their assigned equipment. The dispatcher announced it on the radio. "KMN-909 Nelsonville Fire Department, this is an all-call. We have a report of a structure fire in the downtown. I repeat, a structure fire in the downtown area."

The air hung heavy, thick with smoke that clung to the town like dry ice in a horror film. The temperature hovered around sixty-five degrees as we rounded the corner, the fire engine's tires gripping the pavement. My foot trembled nervously as I expertly maneuvered the engine into position, its red bulk casting a shadow over the cobblestone square.

Before us stood Stuart's Opera House—a grand three-story structure that stretched half a block. Its imposing facade extended to the neighboring residential buildings, a testament to its significance in our small town. Four stories high, it housed not only the stage area but also the dreams and memories of generations.

George Stuart, the visionary behind this cultural gem, had once operated a showboat. In 1879, he transformed that vision into reality, erecting the opera house that would become Nelsonville's beating heart. Within its walls, entertainment shows dazzled audiences, community events fostered camaraderie, and high school graduations marked the passage of time.

As the smoke swirled around us, I knew that this was no ordinary fire. It threatened more than just bricks and mortar—it threatened our shared history, our collective soul. With determination etched on our faces, we charged forward, ready to battle the flames and protect the heart of our town during the coal mining boom in the nineteenth century. Nelsonville thrived, and Stuart's Opera House stood as a testament to the town's establishment and prosperity. Five small shops were on the bottom story, and there was a foyer for the ticket area and a waiting area inside. Washington Street was to the north, and the town square was on the west. The Appalachian City of Nelsonville had five thousand residents, and the coverage area included three townships that totaled more than twelve thousand. It had seen structure fires before, but this was going to be a big one, and a rather large crowd was forming.

Amid the chaos of smoke and flames, Steve—a seasoned firefighter—grappled with the stubborn two-and-one-half-inch hose. The nearest hydrant lay across the street, its metal mouth waiting to unleash a torrent of water. Steve's muscles strained as he pulled the hose, its rubber resisting like a wild animal refusing to be tamed. Two hundred feet of tension stretched between him and the hydrant, and exhaustion etched lines on his face.

Finally, he reached the plug, unscrewing it with the precision of a surgeon. The hydrant wrench clanked against metal, and he secured the hose, sweat-soaked and determined. As he glanced up at me, his eyes held a silent question: "Are you ready?"

I had my own task—connecting the hose to the engine. With a swift motion, I fixed the broken fitting and signaled to Steve. His thumbs-up triggered the next crucial step. He cranked the hydrant, and water surged through the hose, its journey marked by a rhythmic popping sound as it hit each wrinkle. The engine's pump roared to life, its weight pulling downward—a tangible declaration of readiness.

The firefighters stood shoulder to shoulder, adrenaline coursing through their veins. The dragon of fire awaited them, but their resolve remained unwavering. In that charged moment, they were more than individuals—they were a team, bound by duty and fueled by courage. I looked up at the large structure, with smoke billowing out of every orifice. The top levels had smoke coming from the bottoms and tops of the windows, even though they were not broken. The building looked like a large living dragon that was ready to belch fire and brimstone down upon us. Without more help, we could certainly not fight a fire this big. The ladder truck pulled up close to the engine and started laying its lines. The captain jumped from the truck and looked at the situation. He had been with the department for fifteen years and was the most experienced on the team at the time. He immediately radioed in and asked for a second alarm.

He told the dispatcher to alert any department for assistance.

In the heart of Lancaster, a city of fifty-two thousand souls, the Fire Department hummed with its daily routines—laundry cycles and meal preparations. Station 1, one of three, buzzed with activity as an eight-person crew manned their posts. Our fire department had forged an unspoken brotherhood with them, a bond born from shared training and a common purpose.

Four months earlier, when the streets buzzed with life, I found myself at the Lancaster Fire Department for my recruit training—a far cry from my small-town roots in Nelsonville. Lancaster was a city of fifty thousand souls, bustling with activity. Three fire stations stood sentinel, their red trucks poised for action. It was a world of difference from the cozy familiarity of my hometown.

As the only outsider among twelve new recruits, I felt like an intruder—an imposter in their tight-knit fraternity. But the seasoned firefighters welcomed me, their camaraderie bridging the gap. They taught me the ropes and shared stories of bravery and loss, and soon I was no longer an outsider. I was one of their own—a firefighter, bound by duty and honor.

The dispatch at Lancaster Fire Department monitored radio traffic, and on that fateful day, it piped in the urgent calls from our fire. Among those on duty was Sam Price, a recruit who had trained alongside me. Sam's demeanor was pleasant and cheerful, yet beneath his quiet exterior burned a fierce determination to become a firefighter. Since boyhood, he'd harbored dreams of this noble service, and now, as he neared the end of his probationary period, retirement seemed like a distant but cherished goal.

As the call echoed across the airwaves, neighboring departments sprang into action. Athens, York Township, Starr Township, Logan, Berne Township, and New Straitsville all mobilized their equipment and firefighters. Athens and Lancaster dispatched ladder companies, their engines racing toward the unfolding disaster. Lancaster, without a formal mutual aid contract, extended a helping hand anyway—a testament to the unbreakable bonds that unite those who stand ready to battle the flames. More and more firefighters were arriving, along with the Chief Knight of the Nelsonville Department. He started giving assignments and divided firefighters into companies. As the Chief arrived at our engine, he instructed Steve and me to join the two Lancaster firefighters that had arrived, and the Chief told us to go to the back of the building with ladders and protect the back exposures from what would certainly be a threat from the inferno.

When firefighters respond to incidents, riding assignments play a crucial role in coordinating their actions and ensuring effective operations. These assignments define the roles of each crew member based on their seat position within the apparatus.

Let's break down the riding assignments for the first-due truck company in a typical scenario like the one described: The company officer (usually a captain) sits in the A seat (front passenger seat). Their responsibility includes conducting a size-up upon arrival. This size-up sets the stage for the entire incident. The captain communicates clearly and calmly over the radio, providing essential information (e.g., a two-story wood frame, smoke showing from the B/C corner). This initial assessment guides subsequent actions by other crews: (1) the B seat (directly behind the A seat, facing forward) is assigned to the irons (tools used for forcible entry and search); (2) the C seat (directly behind the driver, facing forward) is assigned to the hook and can (tools for ventilation and forcible entry). These firefighters work together to force doors, breach walls, and perform other critical tasks. The driver operates the apparatus and ensures its positioning. While not directly involved in firefighting tasks, the driver's role is essential for water supply, positioning, and safe movement of the truck. These riding assignments provide clear expectations for each crew member, allowing them to work efficiently without constant micromanagement. When everyone knows their role, it minimizes radio communications, reduces freelancing, and enhances overall safety on the scene. However, breaking from this standard role, we grabbed our equipment and headed around the back of the structure.

Four figures stood poised at the edge of chaos, their breathing labored. The fire station loomed behind them, its red-brick facade a stark contrast to the flickering orange inferno that consumed the building ahead. Steve and Sam, seasoned firefighters, strained against the weight of the aluminum ladder. It was a beast—a thirty-five-foot behemoth that had seen countless rescues, its rungs worn smooth by gloved hands. The ladder truck groaned in protest as they wrestled it into position. Steve's face was etched with determination, while Sam's eyes flickered with adrenaline-fueled urgency.

Beside them, I stood gripping a pike pole—a long, gnarled staff with a wicked hook at one end. Its wooden handle was worn, and the varnish chipped from years of use. My fingers traced the grooves, memories of past battles etched into the grain. The pike pole was my lifeline, my connection to the heart of the blaze.

And then there was the handline—a lifeline of a different kind. A one-and-one-half-inch hose coiled at my feet, its rubber casing warm and pliant. I could feel the pulse of water coursing through it, ready to surge forth at my command. The nozzle was my weapon, my shield against the flames that danced hungrily before us.

Together, we moved as one—a symphony of purpose. Steve and Sam hoisted the ladder, its weight shifting the balance of the universe. I followed, pike pole in hand, eyes fixed on the building's upper windows. The fire roared, its crackling fury drowning out all other sounds. We were a trio of warriors, bound by duty and the unspoken promise to protect.

As we advanced, the heat intensified. The ladder scraped against the brick, its metal feet finding purchase on the icy ground. Steve's voice cut through the chaos, his orders crisp and urgent. Sam nodded, sweat streaming down his soot-streaked face. I tightened my grip on the pike pole, ready to breach the inferno's heart.

And then, with a collective breath, we ascended. Steve and Sam climbed the ladder, their boots ringing against the rungs. I followed, my handline slung over my shoulder and my pike pole hooked to my belt. The flames licked at our heels, hungry for flesh and bone. But we pressed on, driven by the knowledge that lives hung in the balance.

Upward, we climbed into the maw of the fire. The ladder trembled beneath our weight, its aluminum frame groaning. Each step brought us closer to the unknown—a world of smoke and shadows, of trapped souls and desperate prayers. But we were firefighters, guardians of the night. Our purpose was clear: to reach the heart of the blaze, to quell its fury, and to emerge unscathed.

And so with the ladder as our steppingstone, we stepped into the inferno. The flames roared, their heat searing our skin. But we were not alone. Together, we forged ahead, our footsteps echoing through the crackling chaos. Steve, Sam, and I—a brotherhood of courage bound by duty and the unyielding promise to serve.

Meanwhile, on the west front and north side of the building, amid the chaos, three ladder trucks stood sentinel—their long arms extended high above the inferno. These weren't the modern ladder platforms with remote outlets; no, these were the old-school kind. Firefighters clambered up the rungs, their gloved hands gripping the metal. Each ladder bore a monitor spigot, ready to unleash its torrent of water.

As the nozzles came to life, water surged forth, cascading downward. The firefighters battled both gravity and flames, their determination unwavering. The building groaned, smoke billowing from its windows, but they pressed on. Hand over hand, they operated the spouts, their faces etched with sweat and resolve. The fire raged, but so did their courage—their legacy was etched in every drop that fell.

Fire was shooting out of the windows of the stage area, and the stage-area roof was one story above the windows that were shooting flames from them. We had to ask for another ladder to get down to the roof, where the flames were. We received another ladder from the firefighters on the ground. It was brought up by the thirty-five-foot ladder that we had placed earlier. Hand over hand, it was delivered to the awaiting roof area and lowered down onto the lower roof. Three of us climbed down onto the lower roof, and the one and one-half-inch line was passed down to us fully charged.

The inferno raged, flames licking the air as they burst from the stage area's windows. But the stage roof loomed higher, just out of reach. We needed another ladder—a lifeline to the flames that threatened to consume the building.

From the ground, our fellow firefighters responded swiftly. They hoisted a ladder, its aluminum rungs glinting in the fire's glow. Up it went, carried by the thirty-five-foot ladder we had positioned earlier. Hand over hand, we guided it to the awaiting roof, our gloves gripping the metal with urgency.

Three of us descended onto the lower roof, adrenaline pumping. The one-and-one-half-inch hose line followed, fully charged and ready for battle. As the flames danced below, we stood poised—determined, united, and ready to face the dragon that roared above.

The roof was an inferno—a blistering furnace fueled by the relentless fire below. Heat radiated through our gear, searing our skin even through the protective layers. The air itself seemed to ignite, scorching our lungs with every breath. As for the smoke, it clung to us like a malevolent ghost, obscuring our vision and choking our senses. We fought through both—the heat and the smoke—knowing that our mission was to tame the dragon that raged above.

The inferno raged, flames clawing at the windows like a desperate beast. I gripped the nozzle, my heart pounding in sync with the water surging through the hose. Beside me, Sam and another firefighter braced themselves, their gloved hands providing the necessary backup.

I adjusted the stream—part fog, part straight—aiming for the heart of the fire. The water hit its mark, pushing the flames back into the building. Our boots crunched on charred debris as we advanced, and the smoke was held at bay by the relentless spray. The heat was a relentless adversary, searing our skin even through the layers of gear, but we pressed forward.

Each step brought us closer to victory—the dragon's roar fading as we fought to reclaim the stage area. We were firefighters, bound by duty and courage, and nothing would halt our advance.

The world crumbled around us—a cacophony of splintering wood, crashing debris, and the roar of flames. The stage roof, once a proud sentinel, surrendered to the inferno, dragging fire and destruction with it. The windows exploded outward, shards of glass propelled by the force of the collapse. Instinctively, we dropped to the roof, desperate to avoid being swept off by the fiery tempest.

But our lifelines were scarce—only two self-contained breathing apparatuses for the entire department. We had to save ourselves. As the initial chaos subsided, smoke and flames surged from the window frames, obscuring our vision. I barked orders—an evacuation to the side roof, where the ladder awaited. Clutching the nozzle, I fought back the relentless onslaught with the water spray, the nozzle becoming my sword against the beast shielding Sam and the other firefighter as they scrambled toward safety.

Their ascent through the fire and smoke was a testament to their courage. Now it was my turn. I abandoned the nozzle, my senses dulled by heat and adrenaline. The ladder materialized—a lifeline in the darkness. Hand over hand, I climbed, my world reduced to the feel of metal rungs and the desperate hope that salvation awaited above.

The heat was relentless, searing through my skin and filling my lungs with acrid smoke. I climbed, each step a battle against exhaustion, my arms trembling as I reached for the rooftop. The flames danced around me, mocking my feeble attempts to escape.

And then darkness. It enveloped me like a shroud, stealing my vision. I felt myself falling backward, the world spinning. Panic surged through me, but before I could surrender to oblivion, strong hands seized my coat. Steve and Sam—my comrades—had reached out, defying the inferno to save me.

Their grip was unyielding, pulling me up and away from the abyss. We stumbled onto the rooftop, gasping for air. Steve's face was etched with determination, and Sam's eyes held a mix of relief and exhaustion. They shouted for a stokes basket, a desperate call to bring me down safely.

As the basket was hoisted up, I drifted in and out of consciousness. The paramedics secured me with an oxygen mask pressed to my face. The world blurred—a chaotic blend of sirens, shouts, and flickering lights. I coughed, my chest protesting the smoke I'd inhaled.

In that moment, I knew: Steve and Sam were my lifelines, the ones who defied the flames to pull me from the brink. Their courage, their unwavering support—it was the difference between life and death. And as the ambulance doors closed, I whispered a silent thank-you to the darkness that had threatened to consume me.

CHAPTER 4

# YOU'RE IN THE ARMY NOW

*1984*

Fort Dix, located in New Jersey, has a rich history dating back to its establishment in 1917. Originally known as Camp Dix, it was named in honor of Major General John Adams Dix, a distinguished veteran of the War of 1812 and the American Civil War. The camp served as a training and staging ground for World War I troops, including the 153rd Depot Brigade, which organized recruits and provided them with uniforms and initial military training. After World War I, Camp Dix became a demobilization center for returning soldiers.

In 1939, the installation transitioned into a permanent Army post and was renamed Fort Dix. Over the years, it continued to play a crucial role in training and mobilizing soldiers. Notably, in 1978, Fort Dix welcomed its first female recruits to basic training, marking an important milestone. Additionally, during the Gulf War in 1991, Fort Dix trained Kuwaiti civilians in basic military skills to support their country's liberation.

Although its active US Army training mission ended in 1991 due to Base Realignment and Closure Commission recommendations, Fort Dix remains a vital joint training site for all military components and services. It's a place where discipline, sweat, and camaraderie shape young men and women, transforming them from civilians into soldiers.

For me, joining the Army was a leap into the unknown. My brothers had already taken that path; their lives were intertwined with duty, honor, and sacrifice. As a firefighter at the local fire department, I had tasted adrenaline and courage, but it wasn't enough. The hunger for something greater gnawed at me—an itch that couldn't be scratched by karate belts or fire hoses.

So I made my decision. I approached the chief, my heart pounding. "I want to enlist," I said. "I want to serve."

He looked at me, assessing my resolve. "Your civil service," he said. "You can take a leave and come back to us, maybe as a captain."

And just like that, I was in. I signed up with the recruiter, my pen scratching across the enlistment papers. Three more recruits followed my lead, and the recruiter ribbon adorned my chest—a badge of honor. As a Private First Class (PFC), I stood on the threshold of a new life.

The days blurred into weeks at Fort Dix. Sand clung to my boots, my skin, and my soul. We drilled relentlessly, sweat soaking our uniforms; the sun was relentless in its pursuit. PT sessions were grueling—push-ups, sit-ups, and endless runs. But with each drop of sweat, I shed my old self, becoming part of a larger whole.

Drills and ceremonies became my daily ritual. I marched in formation, heels striking the ground, rifle cradled against my shoulder. The civilians on base watched, their eyes curious, as if wondering why soldiers moved in such precise patterns. Perhaps they sensed the gravity—the weight of responsibility—borne by those who wore the uniform.

Amid the sandstorms and fatigue, I found solace in letters from Sally, my second wife. Her words carried me through lonely nights, reminding me of the life waiting beyond the barracks. And then Timmy arrived—a tiny bundle of hope and sleepless nights. His first cry echoed across the letters, a reminder that life continued even in this arid, regimented world.

Fort Dix—the crucible that shaped me. Sand, sweat, and sacrifice—the currency of transformation. I emerged not just as a soldier but as a husband, a father, and a man who had glimpsed the vastness of duty and the fragility of life. And as the sun dipped below the horizon, casting long shadows across the parade ground, I knew that this chapter was only the beginning—a prologue to a story still unfolding.

Fort Lee, Virginia, with a history spanning over a century, has undergone significant transformations. Let's explore its three distinct phases:

Fort Lee was established during the US mobilization for World War I. Its primary purpose was to train an infantry division for combat in France.

The post played a crucial role in preparing troops for overseas deployment, emphasizing combat readiness and logistical support.

In response to the rapid logistics buildup during the Vietnam War (post-1965), Fort Lee intensified its efforts.

The Quartermaster Officer Candidate School reopened in 1966 after World War II, and the training program expanded.

A mock Vietnamese "village" was created on the post to simulate guerrilla tactics and jungle conditions.

Fort Lee also pioneered the local use of automated data processing equipment during this era.

Fort Lee's legacy continues as a vital hub for military training and support, adapting to changing needs and challenges throughout its history. A stark contrast to the sunbaked sands of Fort Dix. Here, block buildings stood like sentinels, their walls echoing with the footsteps of countless trainees. Sweat dripped down our faces, mingling with tears and sometimes blood—the price we paid for transformation.

I missed my family—their voices, their laughter, and the warmth of home. But duty and the thrill of it called, and I answered. Advanced Individual Training (AIT) awaited me—a crucible where raw recruits became specialists. My path led to 76Y—Supply-Weapons Repair. The tools of war would be my canvas and my precision brush.

Days blurred into weeks. We disassembled rifles, their components laid out like intricate puzzles. We learned to diagnose malfunctions and coax life back into jammed mechanisms. The smell of gun oil clung to our uniforms, a reminder that our work mattered—each weapon was a lifeline for those who depended on us.

In the evenings, I'd sit by the window, penning letters to Sally and cradling Timmy's photograph. His toothless grin reminded me why I endured—the promise of a reunion, of arms wrapped around me, of whispering "welcome home."

Meanwhile, in the heart of Virginia, there stood a brand-new Toyota 4x4, its imposing frame lifted high off the ground, adorned with massive thirty-six-inch tires. The soldiers stationed with me eyed it with envy, and I, a proud hillbilly from Nelsonville, reveled in my rugged wheels. Little did I know that my adventure was about to take an unexpected turn.

One sunny afternoon, a group of us decided to escape the base and seek solace by the St. James River. The water was low, revealing jagged rocks beneath its surface. But there, in the middle of the river, lay an enticing island—a sandy oasis that beckoned to us like a siren's call.

"Watch this," I declared to my fellow soldiers, fueled by bravado and a few cold beers. "I can drive my four-wheel beast right out to that island."

Their eyes widened, and cheers erupted as I revved the engine and plunged into the river. The water splashed around us, and for a moment, we felt invincible. The island drew closer, and we celebrated our audacity. We parked on its sandy shore, the truck's tires sinking into the soft ground.

As the sun dipped below the horizon, fatigue and alcohol took their toll. We sprawled out in the truck bed, lulled by the gentle lapping of water against the tires. The night enveloped us, and dreams of conquest danced in our heads.

But when dawn broke, reality crashed over us like a tidal wave. The St. James River had a secret—one that no one had bothered to share with this hillbilly. Tides. The water had risen silently and stealthily until our island paradise was submerged. We awoke to find ourselves floating, half-drowned, in our makeshift bed.

Cursing our ignorance, we abandoned the truck and swam to the nearest shore. Soggy and humbled, we called for a wrecker to rescue our once-mighty Toyota. It was towed away, its tires still caked with river mud, and deposited at the repair shop.

From that day on, I learned to respect more than just the power of my 4×4. Tides, it turns out, could humble even the proudest hillbilly. And as the sun set on our misadventure, I vowed never to underestimate the forces of nature—or the allure of an island in the middle of a river.

Six weeks passed—a blur of drills, manuals, and camaraderie. And then orders arrived: back to my unit. I stood on the parade ground, my boots polished, and my heart a mix of pride and longing. Fort Lee had etched its mark on my soul—a place where sweat and sacrifice forged bonds stronger than steel.

As I boarded the transport, I glanced back at the block buildings. They held memories—the clatter of tools, the late-night study sessions, the shared laughter that eased the ache of separation. And as the wheels turned, carrying me toward my unit, I knew that Fort Lee was more than a waypoint—it was a chapter in my story, a bridge between who I was and who I would become.

In the rugged terrain of Rio Rancho, New Mexico, I found myself at the wheel of a military bus, shuttling off-duty soldiers through the winding mountain roads. The sun beat down relentlessly, and the air inside the bus was thick with the smell of alcohol and laughter.

As we climbed higher, the road narrowed, and the landscape grew more treacherous. On one side, a steep ravine threatened to swallow us whole; on the other, a sheer cliff loomed. The wheels bumped over rocks, and I held my breath, praying that we wouldn't tip over the edge.

The soldiers, blissfully unaware or too intoxicated to care, cheered and whooped. They clung to their beers and bags, their faces flushed with excitement. I gripped the steering wheel, my heart racing, wondering how I'd explain this reckless detour to my superiors.

At last, we reached the summit—a barren plateau with nothing but a turnaround point. I maneuvered the bus, sweat soaking my uniform, and began the descent. Rocks tumbled down the ravine, and I prayed that our luck would hold.

As we rumbled back toward the base, I vowed never to take an impromptu mountain road again. But deep down, I knew that this wild ride would be a story I'd tell for years to come—a tale of daring, danger, and the camaraderie of soldiers who laughed in the face of fear.

I had always been drawn to danger—the way it made me feel, consuming everything in my path. It was no surprise that I joined the fire department straight out of high school. For years, I battled infernos, saved lives, and earned the respect of my fellow firefighters.

But then came the call of duty—a tour of service that took me far from the familiar streets of Nelsonville. I served alongside brave men and women, witnessing both heroism and heartache. When I finally returned home, I carried the weight of those experiences—the camaraderie, the loss, and the burning desire to make a difference.

Back at the firehouse, I expected to slip back into my old role as a firefighter. Instead, I found myself promoted to captain—automatic, they said. My fellow firefighters saluted me, and I wore the new badge with pride. But it wasn't enough. I hungered for more—a chance to lead and shape the department's future.

The chief's test loomed—a grueling examination of fire science, strategy, and leadership. I buried myself in textbooks, burning the midnight oil. I quizzed my colleagues, dissected case studies, and visualized myself in the chief's chair. The pressure mounted, but I thrived on it. Failure was not an option.

The day of the test arrived—a sterile room, fluorescent lights buzzing overhead. My palms sweated as I scanned the questions. I answered with conviction, drawing on years of experience and a gut instinct honed by countless emergencies. When I handed in my paper, I knew I'd given it my all.

Weeks passed—an eternity of waiting. Then the letter arrived. I tore it open, my heart pounding. "Congratulations," it read. "You've passed with flying colors." I whooped, startling the cat dozing on the couch. Chief Tim Baden—it had a nice ring to it. I faced new challenges. Budgets, politics, and personnel decisions weighed on me. But I led with the same fire in my belly—the same determination that had carried me through smoke-filled hallways and collapsed buildings. I modernized equipment, implemented safety protocols, and mentored the next generation of firefighters.

Nelsonville thrived under my watch. The community knew they were in capable hands—me, the man who'd risen from the ranks, battle-tested and unaverred. I never forgot the flames—their beauty and their danger. And every morning, as I donned my uniform, I whispered a silent promise: to protect and serve, no matter the cost.

# CHAPTER 5

# FIRE CHIEF

*1986*

In the quaint little town of Nelsonville, nestled among rolling hills, Fire Chief Tim Baden was a local superstar. He stood with intellect, his young face etched with lines of determination and compassion. The fire station, a red-brick relic, echoed with the memories of countless emergencies, and Tim was now at the heart of it all.

Every morning, I would slide down the fire pole, my boots hitting the concrete floor with a purposeful thud. The crew would gather, their camaraderie unwavering. My voice, young yet reassuring, set the tone for the day. "Team," I would say, "we're here to protect our community."

And protect us, we did. Whether it was a kitchen fire, a cat stuck in a tree, or a flooded basement, my team responded swiftly. They knew every winding road and every hidden driveway—the pulse of the town flowed through all our veins.

In the heart of the small town of Nelsonville, where the streets were lined with concrete walks and the air carried the scent of spring, stood the fire station at 29 Fayette Street. It was a modest brick building with a large garage door that had seen better days. But what it lacked in grandeur, it made up for in camaraderie and determination.

At the helm of this tight-knit crew was myself, a young twenty-seven-year-old firefighter with a passion for both flames and fellowship. I had risen through the ranks faster than anyone expected, earning the respect of my peers despite my youth. At just twenty-seven, I found myself leading a team of seasoned firefighters, each with decades of experience etched into their weathered faces.

I believed in the power of blending generations. I knew that the fire service wasn't just about hoses, axes, and ladder trucks—it was about passing down wisdom, grit, and courage from one generation to the next. So I made it my mission to bridge the gap between the old guard and the fresh recruits.

The older firefighters eyed me skeptically when I first took command. They wondered if my youthful enthusiasm would jeopardize their tried-and-true methods. But I was no fool. I respected their knowledge, their battle scars, and their unwavering commitment to saving lives.

"Listen up, fellas," I would say during morning briefings. "We're a team. The rookies bring innovation, and the veterans bring wisdom. Together, we're unstoppable."

And so the firehouse became a melting pot of ideas. I encouraged cross-training—veterans teaching the rookies, and vice versa. The seasoned firefighters shared stories of close calls, while the young ones introduced cutting-edge techniques they'd learned in training.

Hocking College and the University of Cincinnati played a pivotal role in my journey. I attended classes at each college, earning a degree in fire science, emergency services, and fire administration. The textbooks taught me the science, but it was the late-night conversations with my older colleagues that taught me the art of firefighting—the gut feeling when a structure was about to collapse, the way smoke whispered secrets, and the adrenaline surge when lives hung in the balance.

My leadership extended beyond the fireground. I insisted that every driver smile and wave at passersby during their shifts. "We're not just firefighters," I'd say. "We're part of this community." And so the fire engines became symbols of hope, their sirens singing a reassuring melody to frightened children and worried parents.

The fire station also hosted regular open houses. Families flocked to see the gleaming engines, try on helmets, and meet the heroes behind the turnout gear. The crew grilled hot dogs, demonstrated lifesaving techniques, and answered questions. The kids would leave with plastic fire helmets, wide-eyed and dreaming of one day wearing the real thing.

Word spread. The fire station wasn't just a place to fight fires; it was a beacon of trust, a sanctuary where neighbors knew they were safe. The older firefighters, once skeptical, now stood shoulder to shoulder with me, their laughter echoing off the station walls.

And so the firehouse brotherhood thrived—a blend of old-school grit and youthful determination. My belief had paid off: the seasoned firefighters hadn't lost their conviction, and the rookies hadn't forgotten their roots. Together, they faced flames, pulled victims from wrecks, and saved lives. They were more than a team; they were a family forged in smoke and sacrifice.

As the sun dipped below the horizon, casting a warm glow on the old garage door, I stood outside, watching my crew return from a call. They were tired, but their eyes sparkled with purpose. I knew then that I had made the right choice—to honor tradition while embracing change. And as the firehouse lights flickered to life, I whispered, "We have got this, brothers. Always."

The Nelsonville Fire Department was more than just a team of firefighters—it was a brotherhood forged in flames. Their firehouse stood on the corner of Canal Street, its old garage doors worn from years of service. And on that fateful morning, as the sun peeked over the horizon, the alarm bell echoed through the station, jolting everyone into action.

I, the fire chief, with my youthful stature, sprinted down the stairs from my office atop the dayroom. The loudspeaker crackled, announcing a fire at the old train station roundhouse. The Hocking Valley Scenic Railway had long abandoned the place, leaving behind a maze of forgotten barrels—some filled with liquids, others with mysterious solids. The danger was palpable.

I jumped into the car, lights flashing and sirens wailing. As I turned onto Railroad Street, smoke billowed on the horizon, flames dancing like angry spirits. The first engine roared ahead, but I knew they needed backup. I radioed the Athens Fire Department, requesting their Hazmat Team. Chief Harris assured me they were on route.

At the scene, I set up a makeshift command post. But I needed another set of eyes—a fresh perspective. Chief Harris arrived, his weathered face etched with experience. "What do we have?" he asked, scanning the inferno.

I pointed toward the flames. "Unknown chemicals. Abandoned roundhouse. We misjudged the initial attack. The first crew got too close, and—"

Before he could finish, an explosion rocked the ground. The crew stumbled, their bunker gear absorbing the shock. They scrambled to safety, adrenaline pushing them beyond exhaustion. I directed them to the staging area, checking for injuries. The abandoned fire truck sat nearby, abandoned itself—a casualty of the chaos.

As the Hazmat team arrived, I briefed them. Air packs, level one suits—the works. They moved with precision and their faces were determined. Meanwhile, the safety service director appeared, his suit crisp and his authority unquestioned. "Get that truck back in action!" he barked.

My jaw tightened. "Not until we're ready," I replied. "This isn't a routine fire. It's a chemical nightmare."

The director huffed, but I stood my ground. I've seen too many firefighters fall victim to haste. The brotherhood mattered more than bureaucracy. The director stormed off, muttering about paperwork and protocols.

The most intense moment during the chemical fire was when the first crew misjudged their approach. As they pulled up too close to the flames, an unexpected explosion knocked them to the ground. Their bunker gear absorbed the shock, but the adrenaline surged. They sprinted to safety, their faces etched with determination. It was a stark reminder that, in the chaos of firefighting, split-second decisions could mean life or death. The brotherhood held strong, and we adjusted our tactics, ensuring no one else fell victim to haste.

The battle raged on. The fire licked at the sky, stubborn and relentless. Our team fought with grit, each hose weaving patterns of salvation. The Hazmat Team neutralized the chemicals, inch by inch. And when the last ember surrendered, the team wiped soot from their faces, their hearts heavy.

The safety service director returned, his anger replaced by awe. "You did well," he admitted. "I'll back you up next time."

I nodded. The brotherhood had held strong—the veterans, the rookies, and even the visiting chief. They'd run toward danger, their bond unbreakable. As the sun dipped low, casting shadows on the scorched ground, I whispered, "And so the Nelsonville Fire Department continues to serve."

And in that moment, surrounded by the acrid scent of victory, I knew it was more than a job—it was a calling. A calling fueled by determination, wisdom, and the courage to face the flames, no matter the cost.

Some of the terrible memories never leave you in the fire service. Children are the worst. Burned beyond recognition. Drowning in the river. Life is precious, but a child's catastrophes are the worst nightmares.

In the quiet of the firehouse, the aroma of freshly brewed coffee hung in the air. I sat there, savoring the warmth, when a frantic pounding echoed through the station. The woman at the door was disheveled, her eyes wide with panic. I couldn't understand her words, but her desperation was unmistakable. She fell to her knees, her trembling hands gripping my uniform. "My child," she gasped, "in the river…drowning."

Without hesitation, I flung open the door and followed her gaze toward the distant bridge. Her child's life hung in the balance, and every second counted. I sprinted to my fire chief's car, the wail of a police cruiser close behind. The river appeared deceptively calm, but I knew better—the currents hid treacherous depths.

In the trunk of my car, coiled like a dormant serpent, lay my emergency rope—an unassuming lifeline that awaited its moment. That moment arrived one fateful evening when the river's icy fingers clutched at destiny.

I handed one end of the rope to the officer, securing the other around my waist. Adrenaline surged through my veins as I plunged into the water, the cold shock stealing my breath. The swirling currents tugged at me, but I fought against them, diving deeper.

Five feet down, the rope tightened. My heart pounded as I groped blindly, my fingers brushing against something—someone. The boy's lifeless body hung suspended, caught in the river's relentless grip. Panic and determination warred within me as I struggled to free him.

Finally, the other units arrived, their boats slicing through the water. Together, we hauled the boy aboard, the weight of loss heavy upon us. Back on shore, the mother collapsed, her cries echoing across the water. Emergency personnel worked tirelessly, but hope slipped away like sand through desperate fingers.

The firefighter, who doubled as a doctor, confirmed what we feared: the boy was gone. As the sun dipped below the horizon, casting long shadows on the river, I stood there, soaked and weary. The firehouse lights flickered on, illuminating the grief etched on the mother's face. I vowed never to forget those haunting words: "My child is in the river." They would echo in my dreams, a reminder of the fragile line between life and loss.

And so life's currents carried me elsewhere. Sleepless nights and arguments with my third wife pushed me to seek a new purpose. I found it in an environmental cleanup company, donning my *hazwoper* gear—a different kind of adventure, but one that held its own challenges and revelations. Life, like the river, flows in unexpected directions, and sometimes we find our purpose where we least expect it.

# CHAPTER 6

# DANGER AWAITS

*1990*

The Fike Chemical Site is located in Nitro, West Virginia. The site consists of two parcels: an eleven-acre parcel where chemical processing took place, and a one-acre parcel containing the former Cooperative Sewage Treatment (CST) plant. The CST plant treated stormwater and wastewater generated by the Fike Chemical plant. The site owner disposes of hazardous materials by burying them or placing them in on-site lagoons. Operations at the site ended in 1988, but they contaminated soil and groundwater with hazardous chemicals. The site was added to the Superfund program's National Priorities List in 1983.

Cleanup included removal actions, or short-term cleanups, to address immediate threats to human health and the environment. The immediate threats addressed included a methyl mercaptan storage tank, an estimated ten thousand drums of hazardous materials, three hundred tanks and reactor vessels with associated piping, two hundred drums containing sodium metal, and the Cooperative Sewage Treatment (CST) plant. The removal actions included the removal and off-site disposal of a large quantity of hazardous materials and the dismantling of the CST plant.

The suit weighed heavily on my shoulders, a cumbersome exoskeleton of protection. Encased within its layers, I felt both invincible and vulnerable. The ALE air line snaked from my back, connecting me to the rack of three hundred cubic-foot cylinders filled with life-giving air. Each breath was a reminder of the danger that surrounded us.

Randy, my partner, and I were the frontline defenders against an invisible menace. Our mission is to locate the barrels and cylinders of toxic waste buried beneath the earth. We moved with precision, barrel tongs and beryllium shovels in hand, our steps measured and cautious. The excavator, with its massive arms equipped with blast shields, dug methodically. Plexiglass covers shielded each operative from potential explosions, but fear still gnawed at the edges of our consciousness.

The barrels—time capsules of negligence—had been hidden two decades prior. Back then, regulations were lax, and companies disposed of their waste with impunity. Whole semitrailers had been buried, their contents seeping into the soil, infiltrating the aquifer like a slow poison. Our task was to undo that damage and prevent further harm to the land and its inhabitants.

As team leader, I bore the weight of responsibility. Every decision and every move could mean life or death. We danced with danger, our suits creaking as we worked. The excavator's mechanical arms scraped the earth, revealing rusted barrels and corroded cylinders. We hooked them up, careful not to rupture their fragile shells. The chemicals within were a silent menace, waiting to escape.

And so we toiled—Randy and I—our breaths synchronized with the rhythmic hum of the excavator. We stood back, hearts pounding, as each barrel was lifted from its earthen tomb. The unknown haunted us: Would this one leak? Would that one explode? We were acolytes of caution; our movements were deliberate.

After four hours under the oppressive weight of our suits, we emerged, blinking in the harsh light. Decontamination awaited—a three-tiered ritual. First, we shed our protective layers, stripping away the evidence of our hazardous dance. Then came the showers, water sluicing over our skin, washing away the residue of our mission. Finally, fresh clothes—clean, untainted—wrapped us in a semblance of normalcy.

The days blurred together, a relentless cycle of danger and exhaustion. We emerged from the toxic depths, our suits encrusted with grime, and stumbled back to our motels. The beds were scratchy and unforgiving, but our bodies welcomed any respite. Our minds, however, were haunted by the horrors we'd witnessed—the barrels and the secrets buried beneath the earth.

Women at the bars became our temporary solace. Their laughter and warmth eased the weight of our burdens. Randy and I sought refuge in their company, sharing stories of distant lands, lost loves, and near misses. Beer flowed freely, washing away the metallic taste of fear. But dawn always arrived too soon, dragging us back to the graveyard of barrels.

Week three marked the turning point. Randy's eyes held a thousand tales, etched lines mapping his journey from Down Under to this forsaken place. We suited up, our camaraderie unspoken but palpable. The three hundred-cubic-foot cylinder pressed into my shoulder—a constant companion. Randy carried another, both of us silent and resolute.

The excavators roared to life, their mechanical arms scraping the earth. Randy and I fanned out, scanning for signs of danger. The first barrels emerged—fragments of decay. But then, unmistakable shapes: full barrels, waiting to reveal their secrets. I gripped the tongs, my muscles straining. That's when it happened—a metallic scrape, a hiss, and an explosion. Randy had found a propane cylinder, and its wrath was unleashed. I was thrown, rolling down the hillside, debris raining around me.

I staggered to my feet, checking my suit. Intact. Air lines secure. But Randy? Panic surged. His shredded Level One suit lay ahead; the air line was severed. Desperation fueled my sprint toward him, but my own air line held me captive. Disconnecting meant death. I yanked futilely. His eyes met mine, wide and pleading. "Randy, don't die," I choked out. "Help is coming." Foolish words, but he understood. His gaze bore into my soul, and then his eyes closed, slipping away.

And so I stood there—alone, haunted, burdened by the weight of a world poisoned by negligence. Each day, we returned, our footsteps echoing those who'd buried their sins. The women, the beer, the stories—they blurred into a desperate rhythm. But Randy's absence carved a void, a reminder that some scars never heal.

Randy, like Tippie the man and dog with a thousand stories, left me standing there—alone, shattered, and forever haunted by the memory of that fateful day in the toxic wasteland.

The fluorescent lights flickered overhead, casting a sterile glow on the linoleum floor. The emergency room buzzed with activity—a symphony of beeping monitors and hurried footsteps. Randy had been taken by helicopter to the hospital. I had seen death before—too many times to count—but this time, it felt different.

As a paramedic, I'd become accustomed to the chaos of life slipping away. The twisted metal of car wrecks, the silent desperation of heart attacks, the anguished cries of grieving families—I'd witnessed it all. But this time it was etched into my memory like a scar, refusing to fade.

Randy lay on the gurney, his skin ashen and his eyes vacant. His life had unraveled in a matter of seconds—a collision of fate and circumstance. I wondered about the family he left behind and the void he'd create in their lives. But my empathy had dulled over time, replaced by a clinical detachment. Survival required it.

Outside the hospital, the world continued its relentless march. I am remarried now—my fourth chance at love. But my heart had calcified, encased in a protective shell. My children—my flesh and blood—seemed like distant echoes. I sent money home, a mechanical gesture to sustain their existence. Love had become an abstraction, a word devoid of warmth.

My wife, once my anchor, had become a phantom. Our connection frayed, unraveling like the fringes of an old tapestry. I seldom went home, preferring the sterile confines of my work. The adrenaline rush of new cleanups replaced the warmth of family dinners. She pleaded with me to come home, but I was already gone.

Job after job, I faced the abyss. Air-reactive phosphorus incidents, where the air itself seemed to ignite. Mercury poisoning is insidious and invisible. Train wrecks, their twisted steel mocking mortality. Plane crashes, where gravity reclaimed its dues and body parts were regained during remedy. Remediation sites, where we battled the ghosts of chemical spills. And the motels—those nondescript rooms that blurred into one another, their walls absorbing my weariness.

Life had become monochrome. The crimson of hazardous waste, the azure of the sky, the emerald of hope—all drained to gray scale. I wondered if I'd ever feel it again and if the numbness would ever lift. But perhaps this was survival—the price we paid for glimpses into the abyss.

The sun bore down on the tarmac as I stepped onto the plane in Tampa, Florida. Six months away from home—six months of chasing chemical spills and managing fire watches. The job had become a monotonous blur, each day blending into the next like the endless expanse of the Gulf.

Clearwater had been my latest battleground. Air-reactive phosphorus cleanup—a pool of liquid fire that defied containment. I marshaled a team of twelve fire watchers, their faces hidden behind masks, their eyes reflecting the same weariness that plagued my soul. We circled the phosphorus like sentinels, our existence reduced to a dance of caution and survival.

The flight back to Columbus, Ohio, was uneventful, save for the turbulence that jostled the plane. I stared out the window, the patchwork of fields below blurring into insignificance. The decision crystallized within me—an epiphany born from exhaustion. I wouldn't return. Not this time.

As the wheels touched down, I felt the weight of my choices. I dialed my boss in North Carolina, my voice steady despite the turmoil within. "I can't do it anymore," I said. "The chemicals, the motels, the detachment, and Randy—poor Randy—it's eroding me."

He listened, the silence stretching across the line. Then he offered a lifeline—a promotion, a fresh start in North Carolina. Project Manager. A title that promised stability, a desk instead of a hazmat suit. But I declined. The walls of the cubicle would suffocate me, and the paperwork would die a slow death.

"Good luck," he said, his tone resigned. And just like that, I was unemployed. The airport echoed with the finality of my decision. I stepped into the unknown, the sun still warm on my skin, and wondered if freedom tasted like regret.

Florida faded in the rearview mirror as I drove south from the airport. The road stretched ahead, a ribbon of possibility. I was headed home, but it didn't matter. The wind whispered secrets through the open window, and I listened. Maybe life wasn't about containment; maybe it was about release.

And so I drove home away from the chemicals, the fire watches, and the sterile rooms. Away from the numbness that had crept into my bones. The sky above was vast and unbounded. I tucked my wings, looking into the horizon, and vowed never to land until I found something worth staying for.

# CHAPTER 7

# A NEW LIFE

After years of battling flames and saving lives at the Nelsonville fire department, the United States Army, with its own danger and excitement, and the environmental peril and unrest, I found myself drawn to a different kind of heat—the smoldering heart of West Virginia's coal country. My connections from my youth growing up in coal country led me to a job driving a massive Mack coal dump truck. It was a beast of a vehicle, with its oversize sides cradling tons of coal extracted from the strip mines.

Each morning, I climbed into the cab, the engine roaring to life like a dragon waking from slumber. The truck's metal frame vibrated with anticipation as I navigated the winding roads that snaked through the Appalachian hills. The excavator, a mechanical giant, loaded the coal into my truck after it had been blasted and cleared from the overburden above. The earth trembled as the shovel scooped up black gold, and I marveled at the raw power of man and machine working in harmony.

From there, I ascended the mountain, the truck's tires gripping the gravel as I climbed higher. At the peak, an awaiting hopper stood like a lookout, ready to receive its cargo. I tipped the bed, and the coal spilled into the hopper, a cascade of darkness that echoed the sweat-soaked labor of generations before me. The conveyor belt hummed to life, carrying the coal downhill; its rhythmic clatter was a lullaby for tired souls.

Down the mountain it went, following the contours of the land, until it reached the Ohio River. There, waiting barges bobbed on the water, their hulls eager to be filled. I watched as the coal flowed onto the vessels, a silent tribute to the miners who ripped the coal from the earth. The river would carry our bounty downstream, a black ribbon connecting our labor to distant cities hungry for energy.

And so day after day, the process repeated itself. I became one with the truck, my solitude a companion. The danger was low—no flames, no sirens—but the weight of responsibility pressed upon me. I imagined the ghosts of those who had walked these hills before me, their footsteps etched into the soil like forgotten prayers.

When the sun dipped below the horizon, I returned home. My fourth wife greeted me, her eyes weary from managing our brood of children. They swarmed around me, their laughter filling the air, and for a moment, I felt the ache of adventure and excitement. But it was a distant echo, drowned out by the rumble of the Mack's engine and the scent of coal dust clinging to my skin.

In those quiet hours, as the world slept, I wondered if I'd made the right choice. Was this solitary road the path I was meant to follow? Or did the fire still burn within me, waiting for a spark to ignite its flames once more?

Only the mountains held the answer, their ancient peaks whispering secrets to the wind. And so I climbed back into the cab, the engine roaring to life, and set off again with determination—a lone traveler on a highway paved with coal dust and memories.

The rain fell in relentless sheets, turning the haul road into a treacherous ribbon of mud. I sat in the cab of the Mack coal truck, pondering my life choices. Was this really how I wanted to spend my days—hauling coal from the strip mines to the tipple? The engine rumbled beneath me, a steady heartbeat that matched my uncertainty.

Lefty, the one-eyed driver, stood next to his truck, raindrops sliding down the empty socket where his eye used to be. He'd earned his nickname years ago when a cat scratched him and an infection claimed his left eye. Lefty was grizzled, tough as the mountains themselves, and he wore that missing eye like a badge of honor.

And then there was Hippie. His real name was lost to time; everyone just called him Hippie. His hair hung in greasy tendrils, a relic from the sixties. He rarely spoke, but his eyes held stories—of

Woodstock, of protests, of a world that had moved on without him. Hippie slept wherever he could find shelter, and today, his matted hair bore witness to a night spent in a leaf pile.

The excavator clanked and groaned as it loaded Lefty's truck. The coal spilled into the bed, a dark promise of labor and sweat. Lefty climbed into the cab, his one eye scanning the horizon. He'd seen it all—the deep coal mines, the accidents, and the camaraderie of men who faced danger together.

Hippie, perched high on the mountain, revved his engine. His truck was older, a relic like him, and parts had fallen off more times than anyone could count. But today, the rain washed out the road, creating pitfalls that threatened to swallow trucks whole. Hippies descended, and something changed. He wasn't just driving; he was hurtling down the mountain, faster and faster.

The first washout sent his truck airborne, a metal beast defying gravity. Parts flew—mirrors, bolts, and memories. The second washout was worse. The hood tore free, soaring like a wounded bird. We watched, hearts in our throats, as Hippie hurtled toward us, the truck out of control.

By some miracle, he regained his senses. The truck slowed, tires gripping the mud, and finally, it chugged to a stop inches from Lefty's rig. Hippie crawled out, rain plastering his oily hair on his wrinkled face. He looked at us, unfazed, as if he'd just parked at a diner for coffee.

"How's it going, Lefty?" he said, as if he hadn't just danced with death.

Lefty blinked, the rain mixing with the tears in his good eye. "Hippie," he rasped, "you're a damn miracle."

Hippie shrugged. "Just another day on the mountain."

But it wasn't. It was the day we realized that life was more than coal dust and rain-soaked roads. Hippie's wild ride reminded us that sometimes the road less traveled leads to the heart of adventure. And as the rain washed away our doubts, we knew—we'd find our own miracles, even in the darkest corners of Appalachia.

The concrete company became my new reality—a union job in Chillicothe, Ohio. I needed the work, and the weight of responsibilities pressed upon me like wet cement. Two of my own kids, three of hers—their faces blurred together, a mosaic of innocence and need.

Life was rough. The days blurred into one another, the grind of the concrete mixer drowning out any dreams I once harbored. I longed for the solitude of the coalfields, where danger was tangible but predictable. There, I'd been a lone traveler, hauling black gold down treacherous roads. Now, I was just another driver, my rig a gray behemoth that churned out foundations and sidewalks.

My fourth wife—our union hastily sealed by a preacher—was a stranger. We had nothing in common except shared space and the weight of our blended family. Arguments echoed through our modest home, a symphony of frustration. She wanted more money and stability for her children. I wanted quiet, with the memory of flames and sirens still burning in my veins.

Day after day, I stood under the hopper, the concrete mix raining down like judgment. Water, sand, and gravel—the ingredients of monotony. The back barrel received the slurry, swirling it into a gray vortex. I climbed into the cab, the engine roaring to life, and drove to the construction sites. The load shifted behind me, a heavy secret I carried to its accepted location.

Unloading was a ritual. The receiver's instructions echoed in my ears as I tipped the barrel. Concrete flowed, solidifying into sidewalks, curbs, and foundations. I watched, detached, as the world took shape around me. The fire department seemed like a distant dream—a blaze I'd once chased, adrenaline coursing through my veins.

Homecomings were battles. She'd argue about money and her kids' well-being. I'd retreat, my heart aching for the quiet and solitude. The barrage of words wore me down until I was sick of it all. One day, I left. Columbus welcomed me—a construction company, new faces, and the promise of something different.

Construction in Columbus became my sanctuary—a place where sweat and steel merged into purpose. The days were challenging, and the rewards were tangible. I'd left behind the coalfields, the echoes of fire engines, and the ghosts of four marriages. Death, destruction. Now, I stood on the precipice of something new.

Money flowed into my pockets, a lifeline against alimony and child support. My kids—hers and mine—were scattered across the map, their laughter and tears carried by the wind. Solitude beckoned, but so did responsibility. Should I fight for custody, gather them close, or remain a distant figure—emotionally and financially supportive?

For now, I focused on the job. Skills honed by years of operating heavy machinery adorned my résumé. Backhoes, excavators, bulldozers—they were my tools, my companions. But every journey begins at the bottom, and so I labored in the ditches. Pipe after pipe, acronyms etched into my consciousness: Schedule 40, SDR 35, SDR 60, RCP, DIP. They became my rhythm, the pulse of progress.

As days turned into weeks, I gained access to different equipment. The foremen watched, assessing my every move. Safety was paramount, and with pride, I ascended. Operator—a title that carried weight. Large machines awaited me, their engines roaring like beasts awakened from slumber.

Each morning, I fired up the dozer or climbed into the excavator. Soil and rock yielded to my touch, the earth reshaping itself. The sandbox of childhood had grown—now it spanned acres. The thrill never waned—the rush of power, the dance of hydraulic arms. I was a conductor, orchestrating progress.

And then came the 750 Komatsu track hoe—a behemoth in size. I climbed into its cab; the controls were an extension of my will. Main-line sewer and water projects stretched before me. Trench boxes followed, their steel walls protecting the men below as I pulled them into place. Sloping banks, deep channels—each scoop of dirt held promise.

The symphony of construction had carried me far—from trenches to purpose. As an operator, I'd dance with bulldozers and excavators, shaping the earth. But life had more in store.

Promotions came like milestones on an unfinished road. First, a foreman—the conductor of a complex orchestra. My past education found its place—figures, logistics, and the weight of millions resting on my decisions. I measured twice, cut once, and ensured every aspect of the job was aligned.

Superintendent—a title that stretched my shoulders wider. Now, I orchestrated entire projects—the blueprint of progress was etched in my mind. But safety whispered louder than diesel engines. OSHA's Authorized Trainer certificate adorned my office wall. I wasn't just in construction; I was a guardian of life.

And then, TSC Safety Consultants LLC emerged—a company that I had formed to teach safety to others, a seed planted in the fertile soil of experience. I taught crews to harness their power safely and to respect the machines that roared under their command. Hard hats became my armor, and safety manuals my gospel.

The horizon shifted. Beyond concrete and pipes, purpose bloomed. Each training session, each life safeguarded—it was my legacy. The hum of engines faded, replaced by the heartbeat of responsibility.

But I was not done with construction.

# CHAPTER 8

# BIGGER FISH

*2017*

In the heart of Ohio, where rolling hills met the promise of progress, I embarked on a journey that would redefine my life. It was 2017, and I had just joined a construction management company in Columbus and Akron. My background will prepare me for this. Well, I had all the management skills; I'd built homes for myself and tinkered with apartment buildings, but nothing could prepare me for what lay ahead.

The challenge? A school—a junior high school, to be precise. But this wasn't your run-of-the-mill oversight gig. No, I was going to manage building it from the ground up. The whole enchilada. The walls, the roof, the classrooms, and the hallways—they would all bear my fingerprints. And not just any school—it was a monumental task, a two-year odyssey that would test my mettle, my resolve, and my sanity.

Now, let me establish the scene. Picture an old hillbilly from Nelsonville—me—standing at the edge of possibility. My boots were caked with mud, and my calloused hands held blueprints that seemed to stretch to the horizon. The community of Lancaster watched with curious eyes. If I stumbled or faltered, there'd be no forgiveness. There are no second chances. Just the weight of expectations and the echoes of generations past.

I rolled up my sleeves, squinted at the sun, and whispered to the wind, "Let's build something remarkable." And so armed with determination and a dash of stubbornness, I dove headfirst into the project. Being the superintendent in charge of all aspects of the project is a challenge, even for a big fish like me.

The days blurred together—a symphony of concrete pours, steel beams, and sweat-soaked hard hats. I learned the rhythm of construction—the ballet of cranes, the percussion of nail guns, and the bassline of bulldozers. My hands became intimate with turning sheet after sheet of the plans, my mind danced with architectural visions, and my heart swelled with pride.

There were setbacks, of course. The rain came, turning the site into a muddy battleground. The budget played hide-and-seek, and I juggled numbers like a circus performer. But I pressed on. I rallied the crew, cracked jokes to keep spirits high, and occasionally cursed the stubborn equipment that refused to cooperate.

And then, one crisp morning, it happened—the final brick was laid, and the last coat of paint dried. The junior high school stood tall, its windows winking in the sunlight. I stood there, my boots now worn and my hair grayer, and surveyed my creation. The culmination of sweat, dreams, and sheer grit by all that had taken part.

The community gathered for the grand opening. Parents, teachers, and wide-eyed students stepped through the doors. Their whispers echoed in the hallways, and their footsteps imprinted on freshly waxed floors. I watched their faces—the wonder, the hope—as they explored their new sanctuary of learning.

As for forgiveness? Well, it wasn't necessary. The school breathed, its walls humming with the promise of futures yet unwritten. And in that moment, I realized: I wasn't just an old hillbilly from Nelsonville. I was a builder, a storyteller, and a custodian of dreams.

I stepped outside. The wind, like an old friend, tousled my hair, and I whispered to the universe, "We did it."

The hills, ancient and wise, echoed back, "Yes, we did."

From building schools to managing the construction job at the Central Ohio Transit Authority (COTA), my days were a whirlwind of blueprints, concrete, and deadlines.

But it was the COTA project that truly tested my mettle. Assigned to replace an underperforming superintendent, I stepped into the role with determination. Our mission is to construct a state-of-the-art propane fueling facility for COTA's buses on Fields Avenue.

Each morning, I arrived at the site, the sun just peeking over the horizon. The air smelled of diesel and possibility. Briefings were given, hard hats adjusted, and the day's work began. Subcontractors buzzed around like bees, their specialized tasks coming together to form a symphony of progress.

The fueling station took shape—a sleek structure with gleaming tanks, ready to power the fleet. But it wasn't just about fuel; it was about resilience. Generators stood guard against power outages, ensuring that the buses would never be stranded. And nearby, a new bus washing station promised sparkling cleanliness for the vehicles that crisscrossed the city.

As weeks turned into months, I watched the project evolve. The interiors revealed themselves—brightly lit offices, control rooms humming with activity, and a break room where tired workers could recharge. The pumping station, a beating heart, sent fuel coursing through the veins of the transit system.

Amid the symphony of construction reports, I found solace in the rhythm of progress. Our project manager, a conductor of data, received our updates like notes in a steady stream. Challenges were met head-on, and the occasional hiccup—because no construction endeavor is without its surprises—became part of our shared narrative.

But beyond the blueprints and steel, a deeper longing stirred. Loneliness crept in, casting shadows across my days. I yearned for more than concrete and calculations. Was it the echoes of past adventures that haunted me, or the promise of a future where someone truly mattered?

So I stepped outside my comfort zone. Cafes buzzed with conversations, and moonlit streets held secrets. Perhaps there, among strangers, I'd find a kindred spirit—a familiar stranger with eyes that held stories and a smile that whispered of shared sunsets.

We'd talk about more than just construction schedules. Dreams would spill forth—the ones we could build with bricks and mortar and the ones that danced in our hearts. Together, we'd explore hidden corners—the forgotten alleys, the rooftop views—where life could finally find its missing piece.

It wasn't about danger or the past; it was about the present and the person I craved. Our love story would unfold like a well-crafted structure, with each moment adding strength to our foundation.

And so with a nod to the past and a salute to the future, I stepped outside once more. The wind whispered secrets of resilience and determination. Yes, we had done it—but finding her, the missing piece, remained a beautiful mystery.

As I longed for more, after-work hours flowed longer. I wandered through more bustling shops, where conversations flowed like clothes on a line. I strolled along moonlit streets, hoping to glimpse an allied essence. Maybe, one day, our paths would intersect—there would be a familiar stranger with eyes that held stories and a smile that whispered of shared sunsets. We would talk about more than just construction schedules. Dreams could spill forth—the ones we could build with bricks and mortar and the ones that could dance in our hearts.

Together, we could explore hidden corners of our lives—the forgotten alleys, the rooftop views. A place where life could finally find its missing piece.

It wasn't about the danger or the past—it was about the present, the person I wanted and needed. Our love story would unfold like a well-crafted structure, with each moment adding strength to our foundation.

I would find this person. I knew she was out there. Where? How? When? These were all questions that sent my mind into a panic.

Amid the scaffolding and blueprints, my children became my pillars of companionship. Weekends were sacred—a time to pick them up, their laughter filling the car as we embarked on our "visits." The park was our canvas, and we painted memories with swings, slides, and endless games of tag.

Soda shops and restaurants welcomed us; their menus were a treasure trove of delights. I watched their eyes widen as they sipped root beer floats and nibbled on fries. It wasn't just about feeding their bodies; it was about nourishing their souls.

Four children, two each from different mothers, had personalities as distinct as the buildings I'd overseen. They carried the weight of my choices—their mothers' absence, my presence. Resentment simmered at times, like concrete setting in the sun. But I tried to chip away at it, one gesture at a time.

I showed up early for school plays, cheering from the sidelines during basketball games. I listened to their dreams, their fears, and their heartaches. And in those moments, I hoped they'd see beyond my flaws—the absent foundations, the fractured relationships—to the love that held us together.

If ever another woman entered my life, I prayed they'd accept her—a new blueprint, a fresh start. But for now, it was enough— their laughter echoing through the car, their small hands in mine. Loneliness retreated, replaced by the warmth of their presence.

And so with a nod to the past—those who shaped me—and a salute to the future—these four souls—I stepped outside once more. The wind whispered secrets of resilience and determination.

# CHAPTER 9

# A CHANGE FINALLY HAPPENS

In the quiet town of Granville, Ohio, where the sun dipped below the horizon and the fireflies danced in the warm summer air, I found myself straddling two worlds. By day, I toiled on my construction projects, sweat-soaked and sunburned, while the evenings were reserved for tending to the farm that helped pay my rent. My home was a humble camper, perched on the edge of the property, its aluminum walls echoing with solitude.

But one day, curiosity tugged at me like a persistent breeze. I opened Facebook, hoping to reconnect with old classmates and perhaps rekindle forgotten bonds. And there, amid the digital sea of faces, I stumbled upon Judy's profile. She was married and still lives in Nelsonville, a town not too far from Granville. Memories surged forth—the days when she was my high school sweetheart, her laughter echoing in the hallways, her shy smile lighting up my world.

I messaged her, and to my surprise, she responded almost instantly. Our conversations flowed like a gentle stream, polite and nostalgic. We exchanged stories of our lives—the twists and turns that had led us away from each other. Goodbyes were said, but the next day, I messaged her again. And again. Days blurred into weeks, and our virtual connection deepened.

Finally, I gathered the courage to ask her if she wanted to meet in person. She agreed, and we set a date—a Friday at the Granville filling station. As the appointed hour approached, my heart raced. I hadn't seen Judy since my firefighting days, when she worked across the street at the shoe factory in Nelsonville. Back then, I'd catch glimpses of her in Kroger, but her husband was always by her side, a silent sentinel.

And then she arrived—a tiny figure stepping out of a car, her sandy blond hair catching the fading sunlight. Judy was prettier than ever, though she didn't see it herself. The shoe factory had toughened her and made her bolder. As she walked toward me with grace and ease in every step, her smile was both a balm and an ache. I'd grown since high school—now a towering six feet, 240 pounds—but next to her five-foot, four-inch frame, I felt like a gentle giant.

I pulled her close, enveloping her in a hug as if cradling a fragile bird. We spent hours at that filling station, catching up on old and new times. Her eyes held mine, and in their depths, I glimpsed the longing—the desire for change. Judy was trying to break free from her marriage, and I, too, sought transformation from my old marriage, which I needed to annul. In that quiet corner of Granville, we stood on the precipice of something unknown, hearts beating in sync, possibly to rewrite our stories. She left only to promise a return.

Our next exciting time together. The roar of the Yamaha Road Star XV1700 Silverado's engine echoed through the winding roads as Judy clung to me, her arms wrapped around my waist. The wind tousled her sandy blond hair, and I could feel her excitement—the thrill of freedom that only a motorcycle ride could provide.

We explored the countryside, the Silverado effortlessly devouring miles. The saddlebags held our hopes and dreams, and the windscreen shielded us from the elements. Judy's laughter mixed with the engine's growl, and for a moment, it felt like we were flying—escaping the mundane and hurtling toward something new.

As the sun dipped below the horizon, we found a secluded park—a pocket of nature untouched by time. I parked the bike, and Judy swung her leg over, her eyes alight with wonder. "I wish I could ride forever," she said, her voice carrying a hint of longing.

I stepped toward her, my heart pounding. Judy was more than a memory now; she was flesh and warmth, standing before me. Her eyes—those big, round, beautiful eyes—held mine, and in that shared gaze, we bridged the years apart. I put my arm around her, drawing her close, and our lips met—a kiss that tasted of nostalgia and possibility.

On that chilly day, wrapped in each other's arms, we made love under the evening sun. Our bodies moved in rhythm, a dance of longing and surrender. Judy's tears mixed with the lake's gentle waves. She tasted freedom and love, but also uncertainty.

The love was a clandestine flame, burning brighter than the sun that reflected off the lake's surface. Judy's heart wrestled with the weight of her responsibilities—the grown children, the debts, and the life she had built. But in the quiet moments stolen from me, she found solace. The trailer by the lake became our sanctuary, a place where time stood still and the world outside ceased to exist.

As summer waned, so did Judy's patience. She yearned for more—a chance to break free from the mundane routine and rewrite her story. Her husband, oblivious to her secret rendezvous, continued his part-time jobs while she toiled at Ohio University. The union wages were her lifeline, but they also bound her to a life she no longer desired.

One evening, as the sun dipped below the horizon, casting a warm glow on the water, Judy and I sat on the grassy knoll near the rock. Our fingers entwined. We spoke of dreams and whispered promises. I traced the lines of her face, mapping out a future where we wouldn't have to steal moments anymore.

"I want to leave," Judy confessed, her voice barely audible. "But my children—what will they think?"

I kissed her forehead, my lips lingering. "They'll understand. We deserve happiness, Judy."

And so we hatched a plan. Judy would move in with me in that tiny trailer, pay off her debts, and leave her husband. The trailer would become our permanent refuge, a cocoon where our love could flourish. We'd find a way together to build a life away from judgmental eyes.

But life rarely follows scripts. As time passed, Judy's resolve wavered. Fear clung to her like dew on the morning grass. What if her children disowned her? What if she lost everything—the security, the stability? She put this out of her mind and moved on, determined and resilient.

The next morning, as the sun peeked through the trailer's window, Judy faced her reflection. Her eyes, once locked with mine in silent understanding, now mirrored doubt. She thought of her grown children—their laughter, their milestones. Could she abandon them?

I, her lover, stirred, pulling her close. "We can do this," I whispered. "Together."

Our love blossomed in the quiet corners of that tiny trailer, where the walls held our whispered secrets and the creaking floorboards bore witness to our passion. Judy's heart, once torn between duty and desire, now beats in sync with mine. We were rewriting our stories—one stolen kiss, one shared dream at a time.

As the seasons turned, our lives settled into a rhythm. Judy's days at Ohio University were punctuated by the anticipation of my arrival. She'd watch the clock, counting down the minutes until she could escape the dormitory where she cleaned and the mundane routine. And when I finally walked through the door, her heart skipped a beat. My rough hands held hers, weathered by years of labor, yet tender as they traced the lines on her palm.

Construction management kept me busy, but I always made time for her. We'd drive into town hand in hand, seeking out hidden diners and hole-in-the-wall cafes. Our laughter echoed through the streets as we ate our meals—the taste of freedom and love intertwined. Then, back in our cozy haven, we'd make love with a fervor that defied our age. Our bodies, etched with memories and longing, found solace in each other.

On weekends, we would escape the confines of the trailer. The motorcycle roared to life, carrying us along winding roads, the wind whipping through our hair. We'd explore forgotten towns, our laughter echoing across open fields. But when we returned, the absence of children hung heavy. The resentment from their other halves was a bitter undercurrent, but Judy and I held fast. We've chosen this path, and we wouldn't let go.

As winter settled in, we huddled in bed, sharing stories of our youth. High school dances, stolen kisses behind bleachers—the memories flowed like a warm stream. Judy traced the lines on my face, marveling at the journey that had brought us back together. We were no longer star-crossed teenagers; we were seasoned souls, rewriting our love story.

And when spring arrived, I continued cutting the grass on the farm and outside the trailer. The green and ripe grass pushed through the soil, reaching for the sun. Judy and I tended to all the flowering plants on the farm, our hands dirty but hearts light. The debts dwindled, and the future stretched before us—an uncharted canvas waiting for their brushstrokes.

One evening, as the sun dipped below the horizon, casting a golden glow on the lake, Judy leaned against the rock—the same rock where our passion had ignited. I wrapped my arms around her, and we watched the water ripple. "We did it," I murmured. "We're free."

Judy nodded with tears in her eyes. "This time, we won't let go."

Our love story unfolded like a novel, with each chapter marked by resilience and newfound freedom. The ink of our past marriages had dried, and it reveled in the blank pages ahead. Judy and I— once bound by unhappy unions—now danced on the precipice of possibility.

As the divorce papers settled, personal properties were divided, and debts were untangled, they stood on the threshold of their shared future. The trailer, once a clandestine haven, vanished, replaced by a larger one—a symbol of their upward trajectory. Three times the size, it cradled their dreams. Judy's eyes sparkled as she stepped inside, envisioning family gatherings and laughter echoing through the rooms.

We moved from the farm to Lancaster, Ohio, a place where our love could bloom without judgment. The shorter commute to our jobs allowed for stolen moments—quick kisses at traffic lights, hands brushing against each other. Judy's daughter, now a realtor, guided us to a repossessed home, a diamond in the rough. For $30,000, we secured our love nest—a place where memories would take root.

The walls absorbed our laughter, and the floors bore the weight of shared meals. Judy and I painted rooms, hung curtains, and planted flowers. The grandchildren visited, their footsteps echoing in the hallway. They had their own bedrooms now—a space to call their own. The dining table hosted conversations, and the kitchen smelled of homemade pies.

Our love story unfolded like a novel, each chapter marked by resilience and newfound freedom. The ink of our past marriages had dried, and they reveled in the blank pages ahead. Judy and I—once bound by unhappy unions—now danced on the precipice of possibility.

As the divorce papers settled, personal properties divided, and debts untangled, we stood on the threshold of our shared future. The trailer, once a clandestine haven, vanished, replaced by a larger one—a symbol of their upward trajectory. Three times the size, it cradled their dreams. Judy's eyes sparkled as she stepped inside, envisioning family gatherings, laughter echoing through the rooms.

We moved from the farm to Lancaster, Ohio, a place where our love could bloom without judgment. The shorter commute to our jobs allowed stolen moments—quick kisses at traffic lights, hands brushing against each other. Judy's daughter, now a realtor, guided us to a repossessed home, a diamond in the rough. For $30,000, they secured their love nest—a place where memories would take root.

The walls absorbed our laughter, the floors bore the weight of shared meals. Judy and I painted rooms, hung curtains, and planted flowers. The grandchildren visited, their footsteps echoing in the hallway. They had their own bedrooms now, a space to call their own. The dining table hosted conversations, and the kitchen smelled of homemade pies.

But it wasn't just about the house. It was about the life we were building—the late-night talks, the morning coffee shared on the porch swing. We paid off debts, saved for rainy days, and learned to love again. Our love was a beacon, guiding us toward a future we'd never dared imagine.

And then, one evening, as the sun dipped below the horizon, casting a golden glow on their backyard, Judy turned to me. "We did it," she whispered. "We're home."

I kissed her forehead, her heart swelling. "This time, we won't let go."

And so we settled into our love nest—the walls echoing with promises, the floors creaking under our footsteps. Life was good, but it was about to get better. We dreamed about finishing our years together in solitude, surrounded by memories and the scent of freshly baked bread. But life had other surprises in store.

One day, as we sat on the porch swing, sipping coffee, Judy looked at me with a twinkle in her eye. "You know," she said, "we've built a beautiful life together."

I nodded, tracing circles on her hand. "Yes, we have."

The next day dawned with a sense of anticipation, the air thick with possibility. I had concocted what I believed to be an ingenious plan—one that would forever alter the course of our lives. I gathered our sundry family crew: her mother, my mother, her two kids, my four kids—all of us converging on the Olive Garden like a mismatched ensemble cast in a romantic comedy.

The restaurant buzzed with activity as we settled into our seats. A crisp salad adorned the table, its vibrant greens a stark contrast to the nervous flutter in my stomach. Judy sat beside me, blissfully unaware of the grand design unfolding around her. I had told her it was a simple family dinner, nothing more. Little did she know that hidden in my car was a ring—a promise of forever.

Midway through the meal, I excused myself, feigning a restroom break. But my true destination was the car parked outside. The matron, ever watchful, raised an eyebrow as I slipped out. I retrieved the ring from the center console, its diamonds winking conspiratorially. Back inside, the matron caught sight of the velvet box in my trembling hand. She leaned in, her whisper laden with excitement: "You're going to propose, aren't you?" I nodded, heart pounding.

Then, as if scripted by fate, the Olive Garden transformed. Cooks abandoned their stoves, dishwashers left their sudsy sinks, and servers abandoned trays mid-stride. They encircled our table, eyes wide with curiosity. I approached Judy, my knees threatening mutiny. With all eyes on us, I sank to the floor, the ring box aloft. Judy's expression shifted from confusion to anger. Her whispered words cut through the hushed atmosphere: "Get up, you idiot. You're embarrassing me."

Silence enveloped the restaurant, broken only by a lone voice: "What did she say?" Panic surged within me. I had to salvage this moment. "She said yes!" I blurted out, relief washing over me as applause erupted. The Olive Garden staff cheered, their laughter echoing off the faux-Tuscan walls. I grinned, but Judy's smile remained elusive. Still, she accepted the ring, sliding it onto her finger—a silent promise amid the chaos.

And so we exchanged vows in the quaint Crossroads church in Lancaster. Sunlight streamed through stained glass, casting dappled patterns on our faces. Our love, once hidden in stolen glances across crowded tables, now stood in the spotlight. We became a beacon for others, guiding them toward futures filled with shared laughter, companionship, and the scent of freshly baked bread—a love story seasoned with surprises and seasoned even more by the Olive Garden's never-ending salad bowl.

Forward Air Corporation, an asset-light freight and logistics company, will expand its facility in Groveport, Ohio, investing $31.8 million and creating 350 jobs.

Forward will retain and use its existing facility in Groveport, near Rickenbacker International Airport, while also acquiring a property at 6700 Port Road. The company is investing approximately $10 million toward the acquisition of the adjacent property and approximately $22 million into the redevelopment of the industrial facility into a unique one-hundred-twenty-thousand-square-foot office space that will bring 350 new full-time jobs to the Groveport campus.

CHAPTER 10

# BUILDING FORWARD AIR

As the dust settled from my last project at the COTA facility, I found myself at a crossroads. The thrill of danger and adventure had faded, replaced by the practical need for stability. Retirement loomed on the horizon, and like so many others, I hadn't given it much thought until my fifties hit like a freight train. Suddenly, the scramble for savings intensified, and my modest nest egg—comprised of Police and Firemen's Retirement, a 401(k), and social security—would barely cover the grocery bill.

Judy and I owned our house, a bargain purchase that now felt like both a blessing and a burden. Relying solely on my company for income wasn't sustainable. So when an email arrived from a headhunter representing a New York-based company venturing into Ohio, I perked up. They needed a superintendent to oversee the construction of a brand-new facility for Forward Air, a major trucking company. The site? Rickenbacker Air Park in Columbus, Ohio. The paycheck? Tempting. I figured, "Why not? I'm a superintendent, after all."

I applied, and the response was swift. They called me back almost immediately, and I dutifully sent over my résumé. The next day, I received the news—I was hired. Craig, the company owner, would be my distant overseer. The project manager, stationed in Rochester,

New York, would rarely grace us with his presence. Essentially, I'd be flying solo: managing subcontractors, liaising with the client, and solving every hiccup that arose. Fortunately, I had a trusty project engineer by my side, a partner in this ambitious endeavor. She was from Ukraine and looked the part; therefore, I had no problems in the office.

And so armed with blueprints, a hard hat, and a dash of trepidation, I stepped onto the construction site at Rickenbacker Air Park. The sun beat down, casting long shadows across the raw earth. The hum of machinery drowned out my doubts. Retirement might still be a distant goal, but for now, I had a job to do—a facility to build, problems to untangle, and a future to secure for Judy and me.

The old warehouse stood like a forgotten relic, its corrugated metal skin weathered by decades of Ohio winters. The city had whispered its secrets—tales of manufacturing glory, late-night shifts, and forklifts humming through the night. But now, the warehouse faced a different fate—one that would test its very bones and redefine its purpose.

Craig's Construction Company had secured the contract, and I found myself at the helm of this ambitious project. Our mission is to transform the sprawling behemoth into a modern office space. The catch? We had precisely one year to pull it off. Time ticked like a metronome, each beat echoing the urgency of our task.

The demolition crew descended upon the warehouse like vultures, their machinery tearing through the metal hide. Dust clouds billowed, and the air tasted of rust and history. We cut off two-thirds of the structure, leaving behind a jagged scar—a canvas for our architectural dreams. The remaining third would house the offices, a phoenix rising from the ashes.

But demolition wasn't without its hiccups. The ancient pipes and veins of the building needed delicate surgery. We saved them, capped their ends, and whispered apologies for disturbing their slumber. The gas service, however, refused to cooperate. It clung to the past, stubbornly refusing to fuel our future. So we abandoned it, promising a fresh start—a new service that would breathe life into our metamorphosis.

Turning a one-story warehouse into a two-story office space was our Everest. The architects sketched, the engineers calculated, and I paced the skeletal remains. Stairs would sprout where forklifts once roamed. Ceilings would stretch, and windows would multiply like curious eyes. The warehouse, once cavernous, would now harbor cubicles, conference rooms, and coffee machines humming with purpose.

The steel beams arrived, their arrival heralded by the clang of cranes. We threaded them through the skeleton, weaving stories of transformation. The walls, stripped of their industrial grime, awaited drywall and paint. I watched as sunlight streamed through newly cut windows, illuminating the dust motes—a celestial approval of our audacity.

As the seasons cycled, so did our progress. The calendar pages fluttered, and I counted sunrises—each one a reminder of our dwindling days. The office layout took shape: glass partitions, ergonomic chairs, and motivational posters. The warehouse's ghosts whispered encouragement or perhaps warnings—I couldn't tell.

And then, on the eve of our deadline, we stood in the completed space. The metamorphosis was complete. The warehouse had shed its skin, revealing a sleek, modern creature. The gas service hummed, the pipes flowed, and the office buzzed with anticipation. We had done it—a testament to human ingenuity and the relentless march of time.

As the clock struck midnight on that final day, I stepped outside. The new office loomed behind me, its silhouette softened by moonlight. I wondered if it remembered its former self—the forklifts, the late-night shifts, the secrets. Perhaps it did. But now, it wore a new identity—a phoenix with steel feathers, soaring toward the future.

The office hummed with fluorescent light, and paperwork strewn across my desk like forgotten dreams. I was knee-deep in blueprints and calculations when the door burst open, shattering the monotony. The foreman, eyes wide, blurted out, "James is down. Just collapsed." Panic surged through the room, and I snapped into action.

"Where?" I demanded, my heart already racing. "Back of the building," he replied, urgency etching every syllable. I turned to the project engineer, my voice steady despite the chaos. "Where's the AED?" She pointed to the safety cabinet, but when I looked, it was gone—vanished, as if conspiring against us.

Years of firefighting training kicked in. Randy's face flashed before my eyes—the fiery explosion at the Fyke Chemical Plant, the desperate scramble to save lives. Tippie, my loyal dog, was struck down at a railroad crossing. I wouldn't let James join that grim gallery. He and I had shared dusty construction sites and forged camaraderie in sweat and steel. I wouldn't watch him die here, not on this unforgiving ground.

I sprinted outside, the foreman riding shotgun in the buggy. We rounded the building, and there lay James—lifeless, ashen. Someone had turned him over, revealing the vulnerability of his still form. I knelt beside him, adrenaline drowning out fear. No pulse. No breath. I gave him a sternal rub, desperation fueling my actions. Nothing. So I began chest compressions—thirty hard and fast, like a desperate prayer.

A crowd of construction workers gathered, their eyes wide. Craig, the company owner, appeared—a witness to this life-or-death drama. Twelve minutes dragged by—an eternity. I continued the desperate measures. Then the squad arrived, medics swarming. They asked questions, and I answered, my voice steady. The defibrillator crackled to life, its electric kiss jolting James. He sat up, eyes wide, as if rising from the grave.

But life is stubborn. James slipped back into V-fib, and the defibrillator fired again. And again. Each shock is a lifeline. Finally, he stabilized, breathing ragged but alive. The crowd erupted in cheers, but none of it mattered as much as James standing there, flesh and blood. No backslapping or accolades could match that moment.

The weight of the day clung to my skin as I stepped through our front door. Judy, ever perceptive, looked up from the television. Her eyes traced the lines etched by stress and adrenaline. "You're home," she said, her voice a soft beacon in the dimly lit hallway.

"Yes," I replied, my voice gravelly. "James is alive. We brought him back." The words hung in the air, heavy with the gravity of life and death. Judy's hand found mine, fingers intertwining—a silent celebration.

We sat in the living room, the fireplace casting flickering shadows. Judy listened as I recounted the chaos—the dusty ground, James's lifeless form, and the desperate rhythm of chest compressions. She didn't interrupt, knowing that sometimes words fail to capture the raw pulse of existence.

"Randy," I whispered, my gaze drifting to the framed photo on the mantel. My brother was lost in that chemical inferno. Tippie is forever chasing squirrels, in my childhood memories. They had haunted my nights, and their absence left a void I couldn't fill. But now, James stands as a living testament—a bridge between past and present.

Craig's call came later, his voice gruff yet genuine. "Proud of you, superintendent," he said. I brushed it off, my humility a shield against the accolades. It was just part of the job, after all. But deep down, I knew—I had wrestled with old demons, pinned them to the ground, and whispered, "Not today."

Judy touched my cheek, her eyes reflecting the fire's glow. "You're more than a superintendent," she said. "You're a lifeline." And in that moment, I understood. Life wasn't just blueprints and deadlines; it was the pulse of humanity—the fragile thread connecting us all.

So we sat there, Judy and I, wrapped in the warmth of our love. The ghosts retreated, their whispers fading. James would live, and I would carry this night—the night I became more than a man in a hard hat. I was a keeper of stories, a weaver of survival. And as Judy leaned in for a kiss, I realized—I was complete.

University at Albany Launches Construction of
Advanced Biomedical Technology Research Facility

## CHAPTER 11

# ALBANY, NEW YORK

The new Center of Excellence in RNA Research and Therapeutics (CERRT) at the University at Albany and the University of Rochester has been making significant strides in groundbreaking research. Led by renowned scientists like Lynne E. Maquat and Andrew Berglund, CERRT focuses on developing RNA-based therapies and training the next generation of New York's biotechnology workforce. Here are some highlights:

RNA-Based Therapies: CERRT explores the immense potential of RNA-based treatments. Diseases like myotonic dystrophy, cystic fibrosis, and fragile X syndrome can be targeted using RNA approaches. Additionally, the COVID-19 pandemic underscored the power of RNA through the development and deployment of mRNA vaccines, saving lives and aiding economic recovery.

Microbiome and Disease: The 2023 Albany Medical Center Prize in Medicine and Biomedical Research recognized scientists whose research advanced our understanding of the microbiome, bacteria, and their role in health and disease. Their work sheds light on how these tiny organisms communicate within our bodies and influence our well-being.

Industry Collaboration: CERRT collaborates with large New York biotech companies like Regeneron, Pfizer, and Curia to develop new therapeutics and establish a pipeline of highly skilled workers in the biomedical field.

In essence, CERRT stands at the forefront of RNA science, bridging research, industry partnerships, and the promise of improving lives through innovative therapies.

The University at Albany hummed with anticipation. The air crackled with possibility as construction crews descended upon the campus, their hard hats like sentinels guarding the future. The mission? To birth an Advanced Biomedical Technology Research Facility—a nexus of innovation, where science would dance with engineering and breakthroughs would echo through the hallowed halls.

I, too, had moved on. Craig's voice echoed in my ear—a challenge wrapped in opportunity. "Albany, New York," he said. "A laboratory awaits—a whole floor to rebuild." Laboratories were terra incognita for me, but I shrugged off doubt. A building was a building, after all. So Judy and I packed our lives into boxes, leaving behind the familiar Ohio landscape. Our compass pointed east, toward the Hudson River and the promise of something new.

Our apartment perched atop a mountain, a sentinel of its own. From our window, Albany sprawled—a patchwork of ambition and history. And there, like a forgotten relic, floated the mothballed USS Slater—an aging warship with stories etched into its steel. We toured it, tracing the footsteps of sailors long gone, their ghosts whispering secrets of battles fought and camaraderie forged.

Rensselaer, our temporary haven, is nestled at the river's edge. I stumbled over its name until it settled comfortably on my tongue. Falls Edge Apartments became our sanctuary—a cocoon where we shed our old lives. Behind us, a seventy-five-foot waterfall roared—a primal force that birthed rainbows and reminded us of nature's grandeur. Judy and I held hands, our footsteps echoing off the cliffs as we ventured to witness the cascade.

But work called. The laboratory awaited a canvas of sterile tiles and stainless steel. I met the client, and their vision was a mosaic of microscopes and centrifuges. We navigated safety protocols, fire exits, and fume hoods. The occupants would be scientists, dreamers, and tireless seekers of truth. I vowed to build a space worthy of their curiosity—a cathedral for inquiry.

And when the sun dipped below the horizon, Judy and I explored. The Berkshires cradled us—their rolling hills were a balm for our souls. The Green Mountains whispered ancient wisdom, and the Catskills stood sentinel, guarding their secrets. We tasted maple syrup, hiked forgotten trails, and marveled at the constellations— our old hillbilly hearts expanding with wonder.

Six months passed—a symphony of blueprints, concrete pours, and late-night coffee. The Advanced Biomedical Technology Research Facility took shape—a testament to human ingenuity. And as we packed our memories into boxes once more, I knew—we had left our mark. Albany, with its river and mothballed ship, would forever be etched in our story.

The sun dipped low, casting a golden net across the Hudson River. Judy and I stood on our apartment balcony, fingers entwined. Her eyes mirrored the silver currents—the ebb and flow of life, dreams, and the promise of something more. "We did it," she whispered, her voice a prayer. "Old hillbillies, dancing with science." And I smiled, for in this chapter, we had built more than walls. We had woven dreams into mortar, and the echoes of discovery would resonate long after we left.

Albany, New York, with its bridges and thundering falls, whispered its farewell. The mothballed USS *Slater* stood sentinel, its steel hull echoing tales of wartime courage. But life, that fickle compass, tugged us westward—back to Ohio, where roots dug deep.

New Lexington unfurled—a canvas of rolling hills and green promise. We bought a plot of land, and the soil was warm under our fingers. Dreams took root—the foundation of our last home. And yes, pancakes. Pancakes that held laughter, syrup, and Sunday rituals. Our garage transformed into a party room where karaoke notes floated and bands jammed. Friends and neighbors streamed in, their joy mingling with maple syrup.

We had sold that Lancaster haven, pockets heavy with profit. New Lex embraced us—a small town with big hearts. Our house rose—a symphony of beams and nails. Judy chose colors—the blue of the sky, the warmth of sunsets. We built rooms for laughter and windows for stargazing. The pinwheel spun, and we anchored here—our forever home. The ghosts of old demons retreated, their whispers drowned by love.

Our grandchildren swirled around us, their laughter like constellations. Our children, transfixed by their kids' happiness, watched as we danced—a pair of hillbillies turned architects of joy. Life's compass wavered, but our coordinates held firm. Amid microscopes and curiosity, we carved our legacy. Our house stood—a beacon, a testament to resilience, and shared dreams.

And when the sun dipped low, casting its golden net, we squeezed hands. We knew—we'd built more than walls. We'd built a life—a constellation of love, laughter, and the sweet scent of pancakes. I was truly a big fish in a small pond.

# ABOUT THE AUTHOR

Tim Baden, currently serving as a safety director for a construction management company in Ohio, has a fascinating life story. Born and raised in the small town of Longstreth, nestled outside Nelsonville, Ohio, he grew up in the heart of an old coal country. Despite facing financial hardships during his early years, Tim's life took a positive turn when his mother secured employment at Goodyear Tire and Rubber in Logan, Ohio.

Education played a pivotal role in shaping Tim's path. He attended Nelsonville-York schools and later enrolled in Tri-County Vocational School. It was during his high school years that he met Judy, who would become his wife. Their bond endured, and they eventually married, sharing a life filled with love and companionship.

Tim's family has expanded over the years. He and Judy are proud parents to six children and doting grandparents to eight grandchildren. Their journey together led them to build their own home in New Lexington, Ohio—a testament to their resilience and determination.

Tim Baden's story exemplifies the power of perseverance, love, and community. From humble beginnings in coal country to his current role as a safety director, Tim's life is a testament to hard work, family bonds, and the pursuit of dreams.